at home
at play

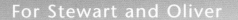

For Stewart and Oliver

First published in 2003 by New Holland Publishers (NZ) Ltd
Auckland • Sydney • London • Cape Town

218 Lake Road, Northcote, Auckland, New Zealand
14 Aquatic Drive, Frenchs Forest, NSW 2086, Australia
86–88 Edgware Road, London W2 2EA, United Kingdom
80 McKenzie Street, Cape Town 8001, South Africa

www.newhollandpublishers.com

ISBN: 1 86966 028 5

Publishing manager: Renée Lang
Design: Christine Hansen
Editor: Barbara Nielsen

A catalogue record for this book is available from the National Library of New Zealand.

10 9 8 7 6 5 4 3 2 1

Colour reproduction by PICA Digital, Singapore
Printed by Craft Print Pte Ltd, Singapore

at home
at play

Food by **Penny Oliver**

Photographs by **Ian Batchelor**

NEW HOLLAND

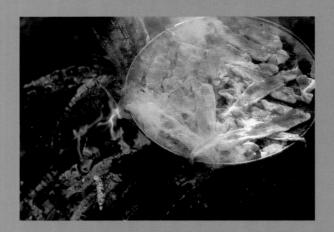

Rain, hail and shine (sometimes all in one day) we are out there having fun. Perhaps it's the remnants of the pioneering spirit, but we just can't stop challenging our geography as we explore the back country – or challenging our bodies as we hit the sports fields.

Our passion for the outdoors is encouraged early as we are exhorted to 'get outside and get some fresh air'. Our own backyards are the incubators for our appreciation of outdoor pleasures, be it kicking the ball about with Dad, the family cricket match on New Year's Day, dangling a line hopefully from the nearest jetty or mucking about in P-class dinghies at the local beach. Later that backyard domain enlarges to include the rivers and lakes we fish, the trails and tracks we walk and bike, the mountains we ski and the oceans we sail.

When I was young we local kids used to take over the street for weekday-evening cricket matches. We would grudgingly interrupt the game to allow returning fathers access to their driveways and homes – and seconds later the dads would join in and competition

tion

suddenly became fierce. The match would continue until last light, when we reluctantly removed the pitch from the road and went home.

Like many of my generation, my backyard activities also included tending our vegetable gardens and fruit trees, and feeding the chooks. One year I took it upon myself to fatten the ducks for the Christmas table. But one duck found an escape route from the hen house and roamed free, swimming in street puddles and meeting me at the gate on my return from school. Dilly, as he was duly named, was of course very smart as his friendship with me saved him. He continued to enjoy his liberty for some time, but then disappeared. I am still uncertain of his fate but I have my suspicions.

A legacy of the tradition of backyard cultivation is undoubtedly our ability to grow outstanding produce. This collection of recipes is designed to make the most of high-quality locally grown ingredients to fuel our active pastimes. The recipes include some Kiwi classics revisited and refreshed, and some new tastes that are achievable, flavoursome

eat up

Replenish hearty appetites on a day of energetic outdoor pursuits. Start with a mouth-watering breakfast of ricotta and lemon hotcakes with banana and smoked salmon. Ease the mid-morning hunger pangs with roast onion or pea and ham soup from the thermos. Feast on tasty sausage and cheese loaf and a tangy bean salad for lunch. Still ravenous? Pot-roast the beef with onions, then eat up and savour.

Roast Onion Soup

1 large bulb garlic, unpeeled
4 tablespoons olive oil
10 brown onions, peeled and quartered
1 teaspoon brown sugar
sea salt and freshly ground black pepper
1 tablespoon plain flour
6 cups beef stock
2 cups water
1/2 cup fresh flat-leaf parsley, chopped
shaved parmesan cheese to garnish

Preheat the oven to 190°C. Wrap the garlic and 1 tablespoon of olive oil in an aluminium foil parcel and seal. Place the garlic parcel and the onions, cut-side down, in a roasting pan. Drizzle the onions with the remaining oil and sprinkle with the brown sugar. Roast for 50 minutes or until the garlic and onions are soft. Remove the garlic from the aluminium foil parcel, allow to cool, cut in half and squeeze the soft garlic pulp into a saucepan along with the onions. Place over a medium heat. Season with salt and pepper. Stir in the flour. Add 1 cup of beef stock and stir with a wooden spoon until a thick, smooth paste forms. Add the remaining stock and water and simmer for 15 minutes. Stir in the parsley. Serve the soup garnished with a little shaved parmesan, and grilled garlic bread on the side.

SERVES 6

Pea and Ham Soup

1 ham or bacon hock
2 stalks celery, finely chopped
1 large onion, finely chopped
1 large carrot, peeled and finely diced
1 large floury potato, peeled and finely diced
1 1/4 cups yellow split peas
4 cups chicken stock
3–4 cups water
2 bay leaves
freshly ground black pepper
fresh flat-leaf parsley
Fried Croutons (see below)

Place the ham hock, celery, onion, carrot, potato and split peas in a large heavy-bottomed saucepan. Add the chicken stock and enough of the water to cover the ingredients. Add the bay leaves and season with pepper. Cover and gently simmer for 2 hours or until the split peas are mushy and the meat starts coming away from the bone. Remove the hock from the soup. Allow to cool slightly, skin the hock and cut the meat into small chunks. Either mash the soup with a potato masher, purée in a blender or leave as is, chunky and rustic. Return the meat to the soup, reheat and serve piping hot with a little chopped parsley and Fried Croutons.

SERVES 8

Fried Croutons

**6 slices stale white bread, crusts removed
about 1/2 cup olive oil**

Cut the bread into small, neat cubes. Shallow-fry bread cubes in olive oil in a large frying pan over a medium heat until golden brown. Drain on kitchen paper.

MAKES 1 1/2 CUPS

Breakfast on Bread

Hot from the grill and wrapped in greaseproof paper, these are great to send the tribe outside with as a convenient holiday option.

6 bread rolls, split open
12 large rashers streaky bacon, grilled
300g spinach, wilted in a pan with a little butter
1/2 avocado, stoned, peeled, and cut into 6 slices
6 eggs, poached
Chive Hollandaise to taste (see below)
1 large tomato, cut into 6 slices

On each split roll place two strips of bacon. Top with a little spinach, a slice of avocado and a poached egg. Spoon on some Chive Hollandaise and finish with a slice of tomato. Grill under a hot grill until bubbly and golden.

SERVES 6

Chive Hollandaise

As an easy alternative use store-bought hollandaise and flavour with chives and salt to taste.

125g butter, melted
2 egg yolks
1 tablespoon lemon juice
1 teaspoon Dijon mustard
2 tablespoons finely chopped fresh chives
sea salt to taste

Keep the melted butter warm. Place the egg yolks, lemon juice and mustard in a blender and combine. With the motor running, very slowly drizzle in the butter and blend until thickened. Stir in the chives and salt to taste.

MAKES ABOUT 1 CUP

Breakfast on Bread

One-pot Chicken Stew

12 pieces corn-fed chicken (drumsticks and
  thighs), bone in
4 tablespoons plain flour
1 tablespoon smoked paprika
sea salt and freshly ground black pepper to taste
3–4 tablespoons olive oil
1 red onion, peeled and quartered, or 1 leek,
  sliced
3 cloves garlic, peeled and thinly sliced
2 red peppers (capsicums), deseeded and sliced
2 large carrots, peeled and cut into chunks
4 large floury potatoes, peeled and cut into
  chunks
1 bay leaf
2 large tomatoes, chopped
1 cup white wine
2–3 cups chicken stock
2 small golden kumara (sweet potatoes) or
  equivalent weight of butternut pumpkin,
  peeled and cut into chunks
200g green beans, trimmed

Pat the chicken dry with kitchen paper. Combine the
flour, paprika, salt and pepper. Coat the chicken pieces
in the seasoned flour, shaking off any excess. Fry the
chicken in batches in a little olive oil in a heavy-bottomed
saucepan until golden brown. Remove the chicken and
drain on kitchen paper. If necessary, add a dash more
olive oil to the pan, add the onion and garlic and fry
over a low heat until softened. Add the peppers, carrots,
potatoes, bay leaf, tomatoes, chicken, wine and chicken
stock. Season to taste. Cover and simmer for 45 minutes.
Add the kumara or butternut and simmer for a further
15 minutes until tender. Just before serving, add the beans
and simmer until tender but still green.

SERVES 6

Pot-roasted Beef and Onions

*On a winter's evening serve this warm and
comforting pot roast with some steamed buttered
greens from the brassica family.*

6 large brown onions, peeled
1.5kg piece blade steak or rolled sirloin
sea salt and freshly ground black pepper
2 tablespoons vegetable oil
2 cups beef stock
$^1/_2$ cup red wine
1 tablespoon tomato paste
2 bay leaves
3 cloves garlic, peeled

Preheat the oven to 160°C. Leave the root end of the
onion intact and quarter the onions. Season the onions
and beef with salt and pepper. Brown the beef in a frying
pan over a high heat in a little oil. Place the browned
meat, juices and onions in an ovenproof saucepan or
casserole dish. Add the stock, wine, tomato paste, bay
leaves and garlic. Cover with a tight-fitting lid and bake
for 2 hours or until tender. Turn midway through the
cooking. When cooked, remove the meat from the liquid
and simmer the liquid rapidly for 10 minutes to reduce it
slightly. Serve the meat sliced with the onions and juices
spooned over the top.

SERVES 6

One-pot Chicken Stew

Lemon, Lamb and Garlic Stew

Simmering slowly on the stove a good stew cooks with minimal preparation and attention. This recipe is no exception and is simply delicious with braised vegetables.

1 large bulb garlic, unpeeled
1 tablespoon olive oil
1kg lamb forequarter, diced
plain flour
3 tablespoons extra virgin olive oil
800g ripe tomatoes, skinned and coarsely
  chopped, or 2 x 400g cans tomatoes in juice
2 tablespoons tomato paste
2 sprigs fresh rosemary
sea salt and freshly ground black pepper to taste
1 tablespoon grated lemon zest
4 tablespoons lemon juice

Wrap the garlic bulb and olive oil in a piece of aluminium foil and roast in an oven preheated to 200°C for about 50 minutes until soft. Allow to cool and cut in half. Dust the lamb with a little flour to coat each piece. Fry the lamb in batches in the second measure of olive oil in a heavy-bottomed saucepan over a medium heat until the pieces are browned. Stir in the tomatoes and tomato paste. Squeeze out the garlic, discarding the skin and stir into the stew along with the remaining ingredients. Cover and simmer for 1¹/₂ hours until the meat is tender and the stew is sticky.

SERVES 6

Braised Winter Vegetables

3 young leeks, coarse leaves trimmed
1 bunch baby carrots, ends trimmed, scrubbed
3 medium parsnips, peeled
1 telegraph cucumber, peeled
4 tablespoons olive oil
¹/₂ cup chicken stock
4 tablespoons butter
4 tablespoons honey
2 tablespoons chopped fresh dill

Cut the leeks into 5cm lengths. Halve the carrots lengthways. Halve and quarter the parsnips into fat strips. Halve the cucumber lengthways, remove the seeds and cut into fat strips.

Heat the olive oil in a large saucepan over a moderate heat. Add the leeks, carrots and parsnips and coat with oil, add the chicken stock, cover and simmer for 10 minutes. Add the cucumber and butter and cook for a further 5 minutes with the lid on. Add the honey and dill and simmer for a further 2–3 minutes, gently stirring the vegetables to coat them with the honey and the dill. Serve immediately.

SERVES 6

Sausage and Cheese Loaf with Tamarillo Chutney

150g minced lean pork
150g minced lean beef
400g minced chicken
1 onion, finely chopped
1 clove garlic, peeled and grated
2 eggs
3/4 cup fresh breadcrumbs
2 rashers bacon, finely chopped
1/2 cup grated tasty cheddar cheese
1/4 cup grated parmesan cheese
grated rind of 1 lemon
1 teaspoon finely chopped fresh thyme
1 teaspoon chopped fresh marjoram leaves
1/2 cup finely chopped fresh flat-leaf parsley
pinch of nutmeg
6 small bocconcini cheeses
plain flour
2 eggs, beaten
1 1/2 cups fine fresh breadcrumbs
olive oil for browning
Tamarillo Chutney for serving (see below)

In a large bowl combine the minced pork, minced beef, minced chicken, onion, garlic, eggs, breadcrumbs, bacon, cheddar, parmesan, lemon rind, thyme, marjoram, parsley and nutmeg until very well mixed.

Divide the mixture in half. On a lightly floured board shape the mixture into two sausage shapes. Press 3 bocconcini into the centre of one half of the mixture along the length and reshape. Dust with plain flour, dip into the beaten egg and roll in the breadcrumbs. Repeat the process with the remaining half of the mixture. Refrigerate the rolls for 1 hour or overnight.

Preheat the oven to 180°C. Shallow-fry the rolls in oil over a medium heat until golden brown. Place them in loaf tins and bake for 20–30 minutes. Allow the loaves to cool in the tins.

When ready to serve, remove the loaves from the tins, slice thinly and serve with rustic bread accompanied with Tamarillo Chutney.

SERVES 12

Tamarillo Chutney

500g tamarillo flesh (halve and scoop out), chopped
250g apples, peeled, cored and sliced
250g red onions, peeled, halved and thinly sliced
1 clove garlic, peeled and grated
1/4 cup malt vinegar
1/4 cup balsamic vinegar
1 1/2 cups brown sugar
1 small fresh red chilli, deseeded and sliced
sea salt and freshly ground black pepper to taste

Place all the ingredients into a heavy-bottomed saucepan and gently simmer for about 1 1/4 hours until rich and soft. Remove from the heat, pour into clean, warm sterilised jars and seal. Keep in a cool dark cupboard for up to 1 year.

MAKES ABOUT 6 CUPS

Sausage and Cheese Loaf with Tamarillo Chutney

Ricotta and Lemon Hotcakes with Banana, Smoked
Salmon and Maple Syrup

Ricotta and Lemon Hotcakes with Banana, Smoked Salmon and Maple Syrup

Spoil yourself and your family or friends on a weekend with this mouth-watering brunch.

1$^{1}/_{3}$ cups ricotta
$^{1}/_{4}$ cup milk
4 eggs, separated
1 cup self-raising flour
1 teaspoon grated lemon zest
pinch of salt
butter for cooking
6 small bananas
400g smoked salmon
maple syrup
lemon wedges

Place the ricotta, milk and egg yolks in a bowl and mix together. Sift the flour into another bowl and add the lemon zest and salt. Pour the ricotta mixture into the flour mixture and stir together until just combined. Beat the egg whites until stiff and gently fold into the batter.

In a large heavy-bottomed frying pan, melt a knob of butter over a medium heat. Allowing 2–3 tablespoons of mixture per hotcake, cook in batches until bubbling on the surface and the underside is golden brown. Turn and brown the other side. Serve a couple of hotcakes per person, with a split banana, some smoked salmon, maple syrup and a squeeze of lemon juice.

SERVES 6

Lamb, Pork and Eggplant Parmigiano

MEATBALLS
1 onion, finely chopped
2 cloves garlic, peeled and grated
2 tablespoons olive oil
250g minced lean lamb
250g minced lean pork
1 cup fresh oregano leaves
1/2 cup finely chopped parsley
1/2 cup fresh breadcrumbs
1 egg
1 tablespoon tomato paste
1/4 cup freshly grated parmesan cheese
sea salt and freshly ground black pepper to taste
plain flour
olive oil for cooking

2 red peppers (capsicums), roasted and skinned
  (see page 74)
1 large eggplant (aubergine)
olive oil for cooking
1 1/2 cups fresh basil leaves
250g mozzarella or bocconcini cheese, sliced
3 cups Tomato Sauce (see page 57) or use store-
  bought tomato sauce
1/2 cup freshly grated parmesan cheese

To make the meatballs, fry the onion and garlic in the olive oil in a frying pan over a low heat until soft. Combine the onion, garlic, minced lamb and pork, oregano, parsley, breadcrumbs, egg, tomato paste, parmesan and salt and pepper in a bowl. With wet hands roll and pat the mixture into meatballs (makes 18). Dust the meatballs with flour. Partially cook the meatballs in batches in a heavy-bottomed frying pan in olive oil over a medium heat until they are brown. Drain on kitchen paper, being careful not to break up the meatballs.

Preheat the oven to 200°C. Slice the skinned peppers into large chunks. Remove the ends from the eggplant.

Cut the eggplant into eighths lengthways and cut into bite-sized chunks. Toss in a little olive oil until just coated, place in a baking pan and roast for 20 minutes until golden and tender. Turn during cooking.

Place the meatballs, eggplant, peppers, basil leaves and half the mozzarella in an ovenproof baking dish. Spoon the tomato sauce over, ensuring it coats all the food. Sprinkle the parmesan and the remaining mozzarella on top. Bake for 30 minutes until the meatballs are cooked through and the cheese is melted and golden.

SERVES 6

Caramelised Parsnips and Carrots

Sweet-flavoured root vegetables are satisfying with weekend roasts.

4 medium parsnips, peeled
6 medium carrots, peeled
3 tablespoons olive oil
50g butter, melted
sea salt and cracked black pepper
3 tablespoons brown sugar

Preheat the oven to 200°C. Halve the parsnips and carrots and cut into sticks. Toss the vegetables in the olive oil to moisten them. Place in a baking tray and bake until the vegetables are just tender, about 20–25 minutes. Remove the vegetables from the oven. Pour on the butter, season with salt and pepper, and sprinkle with the sugar. Toss the vegetables to ensure they are well coated. Return to the oven and bake for a further 10 minutes until the vegetables are golden and sticky.

SERVES 6

Store-cupboard Salad

A simple throw-together one-platter salad using ingredients often found in the fridge or cupboard.

4 hard-boiled eggs, peeled and halved
2 cups wild rocket or any other fresh greens
1 small red onion, peeled, halved and thinly sliced
2 large vine-ripened tomatoes, cut into eighths
sea salt and freshly ground black pepper
$^1/_2$ cup black olives
$^1/_4$ cup pine nuts
300g feta cheese, crumbled
200g any meat or fish you have on hand (tuna, salmon, tongue, sausages, bacon, ham) cut or broken into bite-sized pieces
dressing for serving

Layer the ingredients on a serving plate and serve with any favourite dressing and crusty bread.

SERVES 4

Store-cupboard Salad

Bean Salad

A tasty and nourishing salad easily packed in a container to take into the great outdoors. Other dried beans such as cannellini or haricot or a combination can be used.

$^3/_4$ cup dried borlotti beans, soaked overnight in cold water
$^1/_2$ cup dried black beans, soaked separately overnight in cold water
4 cups chicken and/or vegetable stock
2 cups frozen broad bean kernels
3 small peppers (capsicums), 1 green, 1 red, 1 yellow, chopped
1 red onion, peeled and finely chopped
1 fresh red chilli, deseeded and finely chopped
20 cherry tomatoes
1 cup fresh corn, cut from the cob
$^1/_2$ cup fresh flat-leaf parsley, chopped
$^1/_2$ cup fresh coriander, chopped
$^1/_2$ cup fresh mint, chopped
sea salt and freshly ground black pepper to taste

DRESSING
1 plump clove garlic, peeled and grated
$^1/_2$ cup avocado oil or extra virgin olive oil
3 tablespoons lemon juice

Drain the beans. Place the borlotti beans into a large saucepan. Add 2 cups of stock and enough water for the liquid to cover the beans. Bring to the boil and gently simmer for about $2^1/_2$ hours until the beans are tender. Place the black beans into another saucepan. Add the remaining stock and enough water for the liquid to cover the beans. Bring to the boil and gently simmer for about 1 hour. Top up the beans with extra water if needed. Drain when cooked. Blanch the broad bean kernels for 2 minutes, then drain. Place all the beans, the peppers, onion, chilli, tomatoes, corn, parsley, coriander, mint, salt and pepper in a bowl and gently combine. Cool.

Shake the dressing ingredients together in a jar, pour over the salad and combine. Chill thoroughly before serving.

SERVES 12

Bean Salad

Ginger Gems

You will need gem irons to make this recipe.

60g butter
150g ($^3/_4$ cup) caster sugar
1 egg
1 tablespoon golden syrup
1 teaspoon baking soda
175ml ($^3/_4$ cup) milk
250g (2 cups) plain flour
2 teaspoons ground ginger
extra butter for gem irons and for serving

Preheat the oven to 230°C. Place the gem irons in the oven to heat. Cream the butter and sugar in a bowl. Beat in the egg. Stir in the golden syrup. Mix the baking soda into the milk. Add the dry ingredients and milk and baking soda to the bowl. Mix to combine the ingredients. Remove the gem irons from the oven. Drop about $^1/_4$ teaspoon of butter into the bottom of each of the hollows. Spoon the mixture into each hollow to two-thirds full. Bake for 10 minutes, until the gems are cooked and golden. Serve plain or with butter.

MAKES 20–22

Glorious Golden Syrup Pudding

butter for greasing
150g butter
150g ($^3/_4$ cup) sugar
2 eggs
1 teaspoon grated lemon zest
150g ($1^1/_4$ cups) self-raising flour
2 tablespoons cream
250g golden syrup

Grease a 1-litre pudding bowl with butter. Cream the butter and the sugar in a bowl until pale and fluffy. Add the eggs one at a time, beating well between additions. Stir in the lemon zest. Fold in the flour and cream. Pour the golden syrup into the bottom of the pudding bowl. Gently spoon the pudding mixture in and smooth out with a fork. Cover and seal the top of the pudding bowl with aluminium foil. Place the pudding bowl in a large saucepan. and fill with water to two-thirds of the way up the bowl. Steam the pudding for $1^1/_2$ hours, checking the water level occasionally and topping it up as necessary. Delicious served with a thin custard or whipped cream.

SERVES 6

Ginger Gems

Pear, Quince and Almond Crumble

*The fragrant smell of quince will fill your house as this gorgeous,
rich-coloured autumnal dessert cooks.*

1kg peeled, quartered and cored quinces
1¼ cups caster sugar
¾ cup water
800g peeled, quartered and cored pears
1 tablespoon grated lemon zest
¾ cup plain flour
¾ cup ground almonds
¾ cup brown sugar
120g butter, diced and chilled
ice cream, cream or custard for serving

Cut the quinces into thick slices and place in a saucepan with the caster sugar
and water. Slowly bring the quinces and liquid to a gentle simmer, stirring to
ensure the sugar dissolves before boiling point is reached. Gently simmer for
20 minutes or until the quinces are just tender. Halve the quartered pears and
add them to the quinces with the lemon zest. Cook for a further 10 minutes.
Meanwhile, place the flour, almonds, brown sugar and butter in a food
processor and blend until the mixture resembles coarse breadcrumbs. Spoon
the cooked fruit into a suitable-sized ceramic baking dish. Sprinkle the crumble
mixture over in an even layer. Bake in an oven preheated to 180°C for
30 minutes or until the top is golden and crisp. Serve warm with ice cream,
cream or custard.

SERVES 8

Pear, Quince and Almond Crumble

Apricot and Walnut Chocolate Cake

1¹/₄ cups water
³/₄ cup coarsely chopped dried apricots
¹/₂ cup dried mixed peel
250g butter
200g (1 cup) caster sugar
3 tablespoons cocoa
1 teaspoon baking soda
1 tablespoon warm water
¹/₂ cup coarsely chopped walnuts
250g (2 cups) plain flour, sifted

ICING
200g cooking chocolate
2 tablespoons butter
150ml cream

Preheat the oven to 180°C. Place the water, dried apricots, mixed peel, butter, sugar and cocoa in a saucepan and melt together. Gently simmer for a couple of minutes and set aside to cool. Dissolve the baking soda in the warm water and stir into the saucepan mixture with the walnuts. Stir in the flour. Spoon the mixture into a buttered and floured 22cm ring tin and cook for 45 minutes or until a skewer comes out clean when tested. Turn out onto a wire rack to cool, then ice.

ICING
To make the icing, melt the chocolate, butter and cream together either in a double boiler or in the microwave on a low heat. Stir the mixture until combined and smooth. Allow to cool and thicken. Spoon the icing over the cake and spread with a spatula and set aside in the fridge to cool completely.

SERVES 10

Rhubarb and Strawberry Sponge Pudding

500g rhubarb, trimmed and sliced into chunks
100g ($^1/_2$ cup) sugar
$^1/_4$ cup water
2 teaspoons butter
2 cups strawberries, hulled and sliced
2 eggs
70g ($^1/_3$ cup) caster sugar
40g ($^1/_3$ cup) plain flour, sifted
25g (4 tablespoons) cornflour, sifted
$^1/_2$ teaspoon baking powder, sifted
icing sugar to decorate
mascarpone, whipped cream or custard for serving

Preheat the oven to 180°C. Place the rhubarb, sugar and water in a saucepan, cover and simmer until the rhubarb is pulpy. Allow to cool. Butter a 1-litre ovenproof soufflé dish or pudding basin. Pour in the rhubarb and sprinkle the strawberries over the top. Beat the eggs and caster sugar together in a bowl until pale and thick. Fold in the flour, cornflour and baking powder. Gently spoon the sponge mixture over the fruit and bake for 40–45 minutes or until the sponge is cooked and golden. Dredge with icing sugar and serve with mascarpone, whipped cream or custard.

SERVES 8

Chocolate, Date and Raspberry Torte

Chocolate, Date and Raspberry Torte

A simple cake that looks and tastes stunning. For best results make the cake a day before you want to serve it.

250g dark cooking chocolate, coarsely chopped
250g (1³/₄ cups) finely chopped dates
250g (2 cups) coarsely chopped almonds
6 egg whites
150g (²/₃ cup) caster sugar
2 punnets fresh raspberries
2 tablespoons caster sugar
Chocolate Curls (see below) to decorate
icing sugar to decorate
Chocolate Sauce (see below) for serving
(optional)

Preheat the oven to 180°C and line a 22cm loose-bottomed cake tin with lightly buttered baking paper. Combine the chocolate, dates and almonds in a bowl. Beat the egg whites until they are stiff. Gradually beat in the caster sugar to form a stiff, shiny meringue. Gently fold in the chocolate, date and almond mixture. Spoon into the prepared cake tin and bake for 50 minutes. Turn off the oven and leave the torte to cool. When cool remove the torte from the tin and transfer to a flat plate. Cover with plastic food wrap and refrigerate for 2 hours or overnight.

About 30 minutes before serving, gently fold the caster sugar through the fresh raspberries. To finish the cake, top with Chocolate Curls and dredge lightly with icing sugar. Serve the cake with the fresh raspberries and, if you fancy, a little Chocolate Sauce and dash of whipped cream.

SERVES 10

Chocolate Curls

Melt 150g of good-quality dark cooking chocolate. Spread the melted chocolate in a thin layer over a clean, cool surface, such as a ceramic tile, granite or marble. Allow the chocolate to set at room temperature.

To form the curls, hold a large sharp knife at about a 45° angle and gently pull the knife towards you over the surface of the chocolate. Transfer the curls to a flat tray and firm them in the fridge for 5 minutes. Use immediately.

Chocolate Sauce

300ml cream
200g dark cooking chocolate

Place the chocolate and cream into a glass bowl and melt together in the microwave on medium-low power for 30 seconds. Stir, then heat again in 20-second bursts, stirring after each burst, until the chocolate has completely melted.

chill out

PAPATOETOE PONY CLU
ARENA RULES

- All manure to be picked up from arena.
- The arena must be booked for all jumping & les
- No jumping alone.
- No lunging.
- Long sleeves and a safety approved helmet mus
  worn for jumping.
- equipment must be put away OUTSIDE the a
  mp stands. Poles are to be put on
  cks provided.
- the arena will be available for members
  e at all times.
- oved helmets are to be worn

apatoetoe Pony Club rules apply.

IREAGE - Phone Emma Willson 279-8

USE / LESSONS   COURSES
Members $5 per hour per horse   Members $2 per
Non-members $10 per horse   Non-me

Muesli with Greek yoghurt and honey to fuel a day of activity. A delectable packed lunch of savoury pies and pizza, barbecue balsamic steak sandwiches, crunchy asparagus salad, a slice of lemon delicious or soft almond berry cake. Chill out at home with a sticky Turkish lamb stew and braised vegetables, or spiced pork and quince with mash to sustain the body and refresh the soul.

Muesli with Greek Yoghurt and Honey

A fortifying breakfast to get you through an active day.

3 cups rolled oats
1 cup fresh orange juice
³/4 cup apple juice
1 tablespoon lemon juice
1¹/2 cups coarsely grated apple
Greek yoghurt
liquid manuka honey

Place the oats, orange juice, apple juice and lemon juice in a bowl and soak for 2 hours. Just before serving, stir the grated apple through. Spoon into serving bowls and top with Greek yoghurt, liquid honey and a little fresh seasonal fruit.

SERVES 6

Coffee, Lemon and Walnut Cake

125g (1 cup) plain flour, sifted
2 teaspoons baking powder, sifted
300g butter
200g (1 cup) caster sugar
6 eggs
3 tablespoons powdered instant coffee
1 tablespoon grated lemon zest
Coffee Icing (see below)
walnuts to decorate

Preheat the oven to 175°C. Combine the flour and baking powder in a bowl. Cream the butter and sugar in a bowl. Beat one egg at a time into the creamed mixture, adding a tablespoon of the flour and baking powder mixture after each beating. Stir in the remaining flour and baking powder. Stir in the instant coffee and lemon zest. Spoon the mixture into a buttered 23cm spring-loaded cake tin and bake for 40–45 minutes or until the top is golden and the cake comes away from the sides of the tin. Remove from the tin and allow to cool on a wire rack. When cool, ice with Coffee Icing and decorate with walnuts.

SERVES 10

Coffee Icing

1¹/2 cups icing sugar
2–3 tablespoons butter, melted
1 tablespoon lemon juice
1 tablespoon powdered instant coffee

Combine the icing sugar, butter, lemon juice and instant coffee in a bowl and beat to a smooth paste.

Muesli with Greek Yoghurt and Honey

Summer Berry Cake

A light cake for dessert or to take to a picnic.

175g (2¼ cups) ground almonds
175g butter, softened
175g (¾ cup) caster sugar
175g (1⅓ cups) self-raising flour
2 eggs
500g fresh summer berries (boysenberries, loganberries,
    blackberries, raspberries)
icing sugar to decorate
whipped cream for serving

Preheat the oven to 160°C. Mix the almonds, butter, sugar, flour and eggs in a food processor and pulse together until the ingredients are combined. Spread half the mixture evenly over the base of a buttered 23cm loose-bottomed cake tin, using a fork. Sprinkle the berries over in an even layer. Dot the remaining shortcake mixture over the top of the berries and spread it as evenly as possible. Some berries will show through. Bake for 40–45 minutes. Allow to cool slightly. Remove from the tin. Dredge the top with icing sugar and serve warm with whipped cream.

SERVES 8

Summer Berry Cake

Spiced Pork and Quince

Lightly spiced and great for a family nosh after a day spent in the outdoors.

3 tablespoons olive oil
6 pork cutlets, mid loin pork chops or pork
　medallions
plain flour for coating meat
3 large red onions, peeled and quartered
$1^1/_2$ tablespoons ground coriander
$1^1/_2$ tablespoons ground cumin
1 teaspoon ground cinnamon
1 tablespoon grated orange zest
$^1/_4$ cup orange juice
$3^1/_2$ cups beef stock
2 quinces, quartered, peeled and cored
sea salt and freshly ground black pepper to taste
lemon wedges to garnish
thyme sprigs to garnish

Heat the oil in a large, deep frying pan over a medium-high heat. Lightly coat the pork with flour, shaking off the excess. Brown the pork in the oil on both sides. Remove it from the pan and set aside. Reduce the heat to low, add the onions and cook for 2 minutes. Add the coriander, cumin, cinnamon and orange zest and cook for a further 2 minutes. Add the orange juice, beef stock, browned cutlets and quince. Cover with a lid and gently simmer for 30 minutes. Taste and season with salt and pepper if necessary. Continue to cook for a further 15–30 minutes or until the pork is tender. Serve immediately with mashed potatoes and a little sauce, quince and red onion spooned over the top. Garnish with a wedge of lemon and fresh thyme sprigs.

SERVES 6

Spiced Pork and Quince

chill out

Creamed Pan-fried Celeriac and Cabbage

Creamy celery-flavoured celeriac combines with crunchy cabbage to make a delicious partner for roasted meals and winter stews.

1 small celeriac, peeled and coarsely grated
lemon juice
2 tablespoons butter
2 tablespoons olive oil
$^1/_2$ large, firm savoy cabbage heart, finely
  chopped
sea salt and freshly ground black pepper
$^1/_4$ cup cream

Place the coarsely grated celeriac into a bowl of water with a squeeze or two of lemon juice and soak for 5 minutes. Melt the butter in a large heavy-bottomed frying pan over a low to medium heat. Add the olive oil. Squeeze all the water from the celeriac and dry on kitchen paper. Add the celeriac to the pan and stir-fry for 5 minutes. Add the cabbage. Season with salt and pepper to taste. Pan-fry the vegetables, turning over with tongs as they cook and brighten in colour but are still crisp. Raise the temperature to medium and pour the cream in. Toss the vegetables in the cream for a couple of minutes, then serve.

SERVES 6

Cod, Potato and Tomato Stew

600–700g boned cod or hapuku fillets
$^1/_4$ cup lemon juice
sea salt and freshly ground black pepper
3 tablespoons olive oil
2 red onions, peeled and cut into eighths
1 clove garlic, peeled and grated
2 x 400g cans chopped tomatoes in juice
1 cup white wine
$^1/_4$ cup chopped fresh flat-leaf parsley
$^1/_4$ cup chopped fresh chervil
6 floury potatoes, peeled and sliced
fresh lemon slices for serving
fresh flat-leaf parsley for serving

Cut the fish into six thick steaks and place in a lightly oiled ovenproof dish. Pour the lemon juice over, season with salt and pepper and refrigerate for 1 hour.

Heat the olive oil in a large frying pan and fry the red onions and garlic, allowing the onions to segment as they cook. Cook until the onions are soft. Add the tomatoes, white wine, parsley, chervil and potatoes. Cover and gently simmer for about 15 minutes until the potatoes are just tender. Remove the lid and simmer, uncovered, for 5 minutes.

Gently spoon the mixture over the fish, avoiding breaking the potatoes. Bake the fish stew in an oven preheated to 180°C for 15–20 minutes until the fish is just cooked through. Serve with slices of fresh lemon and flat-leaf parsley.

SERVES 6

Cod, Potato and Tomato Stew

Caramelised Onion and Mushroom Pie

Caramelised Onion and Mushroom Pie

PASTRY
2 cups plain flour
125g cold butter, cubed
pinch of salt
1 egg
about 1 tablespoon cold water

FILLING
2–3 tablespoons olive oil
2 large onions, peeled, halved and thinly sliced
2 cloves garlic, peeled and finely chopped
1 tablespoon balsamic vinegar
150g portobello mushrooms, thinly sliced
150g shiitake mushrooms, sliced
2 tablespoons butter
sea salt and freshly ground black pepper to taste
1 teaspoon grated lemon zest
1 tablespoon lemon juice
$^1/_4$ cup coarsely chopped fresh flat-leaf parsley
$^3/_4$ cup grated gruyère cheese
1 egg, beaten, for sealing and glazing

To make the pastry, place the flour, butter and salt in a food processor and process until the mixture resembles fine breadcrumbs. Add the egg and continue to process, adding enough cold water to bind the dough together. Remove the mixture to a lightly floured board and form the dough into a ball. Wrap in plastic food wrap and refrigerate for 20 minutes.

To make the filling, heat the oil in a large frying pan over a medium heat and fry the onions and garlic until the onions caramelise. Add the balsamic vinegar, mushrooms, butter and salt and pepper, and continue to cook until the mushrooms are tender. Stir in the lemon zest, lemon juice and parsley and allow to cool.

Preheat the oven to 180°C. Divide the pastry into two parts (two-thirds and one-third) and roll each into a ball. Roll out the bigger ball on a lightly floured board to a

25cm circle. Lift this circle into a greased 20cm pie dish so that the extra pastry flops over the edge of the pie dish. Spoon the filling into the pie and scatter the cheese on top. Roll the remaining pastry into a 20cm circle and lift it onto the top of the pie. Brush the edges of top with beaten egg. Fold the pastry base edges over the top of the pie to form a rolled edge. Brush the top of the pie with beaten egg. Pierce the top of the pie several times with a fork. Bake for 35 minutes until golden.

SERVES 8

49

Beef with Pistachio and Artichoke Stuffing

Served hot at a smart dinner or sliced cold for an outdoor feast, tender prosciutto-wrapped beef adds sophistication to the meal.

2 tablespoons butter
dash of olive oil
1 red onion, peeled and finely chopped
1 clove garlic, peeled and finely chopped
1 cup fresh breadcrumbs
4 artichoke hearts, finely sliced
1 tablespoon grated lemon zest
$^1/_2$ cup pistachio nuts, coarsely chopped
$^1/_4$ cup chopped fresh mint
$^1/_2$ cup chopped fresh flat-leaf parsley
1kg piece eye fillet
10–12 thin slices prosciutto

Fry the butter, olive oil, onion and garlic in a frying pan until soft. Place in a bowl and add the fresh breadcrumbs, artichoke hearts, lemon zest, pistachio nuts, mint and parsley. Stir to combine. Slit the beef fillet down its length through the centre, ensuring the fillet is still intact but is able to be opened out. Spread the stuffing lengthways down the centre of the fillet.

Roll back together. Wrap the prosciutto around the beef to completely enclose it. Secure the meat with kitchen string at 2cm intervals along the length of the meat. Place the fillet in a roasting pan, put into an oven preheated to 210–220°C and roast for 30–45 minutes, depending on whether you prefer it rare or medium–well done. Allow the beef to sit for 10 minutes before carving.

SERVES 6

Sticky Turkish Lamb Stew

2 tablespoons olive oil
1 onion, peeled and finely chopped
2 cloves garlic, peeled and finely chopped
500g lamb forequarter, diced
1 teaspoon allspice
2 teaspoons ground cumin
1 teaspoon ground coriander
sea salt and freshly ground black pepper to taste
olive oil for frying
1 eggplant (aubergine) cut into chunks
$^1/_4$ cup chopped fresh mint
$^1/_4$ cup fresh marjoram leaves
1 tablespoon chopped dried apricots
250ml lamb, beef or veal stock
6 medium potatoes, peeled and quartered

Place the olive oil, onion and garlic in a saucepan and gently fry until soft. Place in a large bowl with the lamb, allspice, cumin, coriander, salt and pepper and toss together. Marinate for 1 hour in the fridge. Fry the mixture in a heavy-bottomed frying pan in oil in batches until fragrant and browned. Return all this mixture to the saucepan along with the eggplant, mint, marjoram, apricots and stock. Place a lid on the stew and simmer for 1 hour and 10 minutes. Add the potatoes and continue to cook until the potatoes are tender and the stew is sticky. To serve, spoon into bowls with some greens on the side.

SERVES 6

Paua Fritters

If preferred, stretch this quintessential Kiwi delicacy by making bite-sized baby fritters and serve them as a pre-dinner nibble.

6 tablespoons plain flour
$^1/_2$ teaspoon baking soda
4 eggs, separated
2 tablespoons cream
1 teaspoon grated lemon zest
sea salt and freshly ground black pepper to taste
400g fresh paua, minced
butter and olive oil for cooking
Wine and Watercress Beurre Blanc for serving
  (see below)

Place the flour and baking soda in a bowl and make a well in the centre. Beat the egg yolks and cream together and pour them into the well in the dry ingredients. Stir the mixture from the centre, drawing in the dry ingredients until you have a smooth batter. Stir in the lemon zest, salt and pepper and paua to combine. Beat the egg whites until stiff and fold them into the paua batter until just incorporated. Lightly grease a heavy-bottomed frying pan with a little butter and olive oil and place over a medium heat. Drop tablespoonfuls of mixture into the pan in batches of three or four at a time. Cook the fritters for 2–3 minutes each side until golden but still tender. Serve immediately, allowing a couple of fritters per person, with a little Wine and Watercress Beurre Blanc on the side.

MAKES 12–14 FRITTERS

Wine and Watercress Beurre Blanc

$^1/_4$ cup white vinegar
$^1/_2$ cup white wine
2 shallots (eschalots), finely chopped
1 tablespoon cream
150g butter, cut into small pieces
1 teaspoon grated lime or lemon rind
1 teaspoon lime juice
$^1/_2$ cup finely chopped watercress leaves
sea salt and white pepper to taste

Place the vinegar, wine and shallots in a heavy-bottomed stainless steel saucepan and simmer slowly until reduced to about 2 tablespoons. Add the cream and bring to the boil. Remove from the heat and beat in the butter piece by piece with a wire whisk until the sauce thickens. Stir in the lime rind, juice and watercress. Season to taste with salt and white pepper.

MAKES 1$^1/_4$ CUPS

Paua Fritters with Wine and Watercress
Beurre Blanc

Asparagus with a Pine Nut and Herb Dressing

Spring or summer, this tangy, elegant salad will enliven holiday barbecues.

1 shallot (eschalot) or 2 spring onions
$^1/_2$ cup fresh flat-leaf parsley
$^1/_2$ cup fresh mint leaves
$^1/_2$ cup fresh chives
120g (1 cup) toasted pine nuts
1 tablespoon lemon juice
$^3/_4$–1 cup extra virgin olive oil
sea salt and freshly ground black pepper to taste
about 30 fresh asparagus spears, trimmed,
    halved, blanched, dried and cooled

Place the peeled and sliced shallot or spring onions, parsley, mint, chives, pine nuts and lemon juice in a food processor. Process until chopped. With the motor running on low, drizzle in the olive oil. Add enough to make a thick sauce to your liking. Season with salt and pepper and gently toss with the asparagus. To serve, pile onto a simple serving platter.

SERVES 6

Maple Syrup and Whisky Glazed Ham

Ideal when cooking for a crowd around Christmas time.

7kg whole cooked ham
1 cup brown sugar
1 tablespoon balsamic vinegar or malt vinegar
$^1/_4$ cup pure maple syrup
$^1/_2$ cup whisky
whole cloves

Peel the skin from the ham. Mix together the sugar, vinegar, maple syrup and whisky. Place the ham in a baking pan. Score the fat in a crisscross pattern. Spoon the glaze over and rub it in with your hands. Bake in an oven preheated to 180°C for 30–45 minutes, basting the ham with glaze four or five times during cooking. Before serving, stud each crisscross of fat with whole cloves.

SERVES 25

Asparagus with a Pine Nut
and Herb Dressing

Spaghetti with Tomato, Olives and Herbs

Add some chunky tuna to make this a quick, hearty meal that will fortify those family members heading out intent on weekend sport.

1 tablespoon olive oil
2 cloves garlic, peeled and sliced
3 cups Tomato Sauce recipe (see below) or
**   store-bought tomato sauce**
$^1/_3$ cup chopped fresh basil leaves
$^1/_3$ cup chopped fresh flat-leaf parsley
$^1/_3$ cup black olives, sliced
$^1/_3$ cup white wine
pinch of sugar
600g spaghetti
$^1/_2$ cup grated parmesan cheese
extra fresh basil or parsley to garnish

Fry the oil and garlic in a frying pan over a low heat until the garlic softens. Add the Tomato Sauce, basil, parsley, olives, white wine and sugar. Simmer the sauce for 10 minutes. Meanwhile cook the spaghetti in a large saucepan of salted boiling water until al dente. Drain and serve in bowls topped with the sauce then the grated parmesan and garnished with the fresh herbs.

SERVES 6

Tomato Sauce

2 tablespoons olive oil
2 cloves garlic, peeled and chopped
1 large onion, peeled and finely chopped
4 x 400g cans tomatoes in juice
sea salt and cracked black pepper
$^1/_2$ teaspoon sugar
1 bay leaf

Fry the oil, garlic and onion in a large saucepan over a low heat until soft. Add the tomatoes, salt and pepper, sugar and bay leaf. Simmer gently for 20 minutes. Allow to cool. Remove the bay leaf. Use the sauce in a chunky, rustic form as is, or blend it in a food processor when you require a finer texture.

To vary the sauce, simply add sprigs of fresh herbs, such as basil, thyme, oregano or rosemary to taste while it simmers. The herbs will infuse the sauce with their flavour. Remove them before blending. The sauce freezes well for up to 3 months.

MAKES 6 CUPS

Smoked Salmon, Potato and Goat's Cheese Pizza

PIZZA BASE
1¹/₂ teaspoons dried yeast
pinch of sugar
100ml warm water
1²/₃ cups plain flour
¹/₄ cup olive oil

TOPPING
2 tablespoons olive oil
1 red onion, peeled, and cut into eighths
1 clove garlic, peeled and grated
2 medium-sized floury potatoes, peeled and
   sliced paper thin
200g goat's feta, crumbled
fresh oregano leaves
fresh basil leaves
150g smoked salmon
1¹/₂ tablespoons avocado oil

Combine the yeast, sugar and warm water in a small bowl, cover and stand it in a warm place for 10 minutes until frothy. Place the flour in a bowl and pour in the olive oil and frothy yeast. Mix the dough enough to form a soft ball. Transfer the dough to an oiled bowl, cover with plastic food wrap and stand it in a warm place for 1 hour or until it doubles in size. Knock down the dough and transfer it to a lightly floured board. Roll out the dough to fit a greased 30cm pizza pan.

Heat the olive oil in a frying pan and fry the red onion and garlic until the onion softens and separates. Spoon over the pizza base. Scatter with the potato, half the goat's feta and half the oregano and basil. Bake the pizza in an oven preheated to 210°C for 20 minutes. Remove from the oven, add the remaining feta and cook for a further 10 minutes. When the base is crisp and golden remove from the oven and scatter with the smoked salmon and remaining fresh herbs. Drizzle the avocado oil over and serve immediately.

SERVES 4

Roasted Figs with Prosciutto and Goat's Cheese

100ml water
1 tablespoon lemon juice
³/₄ cup brown sugar
12 figs, halved
2 tablespoons butter, softened
³/₄ cup caster sugar
12 thin slices prosciutto
150g creamy goat's cheese
4 tablespoons avocado oil

Place the water, lemon juice and brown sugar in a saucepan and gently simmer for 10 minutes until the sugar has dissolved and the liquid thickened slightly. Place the halved figs in a single layer in a baking dish. Dot with butter and sprinkle with the caster sugar. Roast the figs in an oven preheated to 200°C for 15 minutes. Gently spoon into a serving bowl. Serve 2 fig halves per person, coated in syrup, with a couple of slices of prosciutto and a little goat's cheese, and drizzle with avocado oil.

SERVES 6

Roasted Figs with Prosciutto and Goat's Cheese

Balsamic Steak Sandwich

2 onions, peeled, halved and thinly sliced
1 tablespoon butter
2 tablespoons olive oil
pinch of sugar
4 portions rump or fillet steak, thinly sliced
3 tablespoons balsamic vinegar
1 small ciabatta loaf
$1/4$ cup favourite garlic-flavoured mayonnaise
favourite mustard
shavings of a favourite vintage cheddar cheese
2 cups rocket leaves
sea salt and freshly ground black pepper
fresh tomato for serving

Fry the onions in the butter, olive oil and sugar until soft and caramelised. Marinate the steak in the balsamic vinegar for 10 minutes and then grill to cook. Split the bread through the centre and spread it with mayonnaise and mustard. Top with the steak along the length of the bread. Drop the cheese onto the hot steak, top with the onions and rocket. Season with salt and pepper to taste. Place the other half of the bread on top. Cut into four and serve with some fresh tomato.

SERVES 4

Balsamic Steak Sandwich

Bacon, Egg and Cheese Pie

To make this delicious family favourite you can use store-bought short-crust pastry as an easier alternative.

PASTRY
2¹/₂ **cups plain flour**
175g cold butter, cubed
1 egg yolk
2–3 tablespoons cold water

FILLING
1 tablespoon olive oil
3 spring onions, sliced
10 rashers streaky bacon, thinly sliced
3 tablespoons chopped sundried tomatoes
10 eggs
freshly ground black pepper
2 cups grated gruyère cheese
¹/₂ **cup finely chopped fresh flat-leaf parsley**

beaten egg for glazing

To make the pastry, process the flour and butter in a food processor until the mixture resembles fine breadcrumbs. Add the egg yolk and enough cold water to process the dough into a ball. Lightly knead the dough on a lightly floured surface until smooth. Divide the dough in two portions, one slightly larger than the other. Wrap separately in plastic food wrap and refrigerate for 20 minutes.

When ready to use, roll out the larger portion on a lightly floured surface to fit a 25–26cm fluted loose-bottomed buttered pie dish. Trim off the excess pastry. Line the base of the dish with baking paper, fill the dish with dried beans or rice and bake blind at 200°C for 15 minutes. Remove the baking beans and bake for a further 5 minutes until golden.

To make the filling, heat the oil in a frying pan and fry the spring onions and bacon over a medium heat until the bacon browns slightly. Drain on kitchen paper, allow to cool, and scatter over the bottom of the pie shell. Scatter over the sundried tomatoes. Break the eggs one at a time into a saucer and slide them unbroken into the pie, spacing them evenly. Season with pepper and sprinkle the cheese and parsley over the top.

Brush the edge of the pie with a little beaten egg. Roll out the remaining pastry on a lightly floured surface large enough to cover the top of the pie. Carefully place the pastry over the pie and press the edges together to seal. Trim off any excess pastry. Brush the top with beaten egg. Bake in an oven preheated to 180°C for 40–45 minutes until the pastry is golden.

SERVES 8

Feijoa and Passionfruit Tart

Feijoa and Passionfruit Tart

A sweet, fragrant, sticky, seductive tart.

PASTRY
1¹/₂ cups plain flour
90g butter
1 tablespoon caster sugar
2–3 tablespoons cold water

TOPPING
³/₄ cup caster sugar
50g butter
2 tablespoons lemon juice
2 passionfruit, halved and pulp removed
8 firm, ripe feijoas, peeled and sliced

whipped cream for serving
extra passionfruit pulp for serving

To make the pastry, place the flour, butter and sugar in a food processor and process until the mixture resembles fine breadcrumbs. Continue to process the mixture while adding enough of the cold water to form a ball of dough. Transfer the dough to a lightly floured board and knead into a ball. Wrap in plastic food wrap and refrigerate for 20 minutes.

To make the topping, place the sugar and butter in a saucepan and melt together over a medium heat. Add the lemon juice and gently simmer for about 5 minutes until it caramelises slightly. Add the passionfruit pulp and simmer for a further 2 minutes.

Roll out the pasty on a lightly floured board in a circle large enough to fit a 24–26cm heavy-bottomed ovenproof frying pan. Arrange the sliced feijoas in overlapping layers around and over the bottom of the frying pan. Pour the syrup over the fruit. Carefully lift the pastry over the top of the fruit, tucking the edges in. Bake the tart in an oven preheated to 180°C for 25–30 minutes, until the pastry is golden and crisp. Remove from the oven and allow to rest for 5 minutes. Invert the tart onto a serving plate. Serve with a little whipped cream and fresh passionfruit pulp.

SERVES 8

Lemon Delicious

For coffee with friends or after the match, this will please the sweet tooth.

BASE
200g butter, softened
$1/2$ cup icing sugar
1 cup plain flour
1 cup ground almonds
1 egg, beaten

FILLING
6 eggs
$1^1/2$ cups caster sugar
2 tablespoons plain flour
$1/2$ cup lemon juice
2 tablespoons grated lemon zest
$3/4$ cup flaked almonds, toasted

icing sugar to decorate

Preheat the oven to 200°C. To make the base, place the butter, icing sugar, flour and ground almonds into a food processor and process until the mixture resembles fine breadcrumbs. Add the egg and process until the mixture forms a ball of dough. Press the dough into a slice pan about 22cm x 26cm. Refrigerate for 20 minutes, then bake for 7 minutes until pale golden.

To make the filling, whisk the eggs in a large bowl. Add the sugar, flour, lemon juice and zest and combine with the eggs. Pour the filling mixture over the cooked base and continue to cook at 180°C for 15–20 minutes until the filling has just set. Remove from the oven and sprinkle with the toasted flaked almonds. Allow the slice to cool. Finish the top by dredging with icing sugar.

Lemon Delicious

Gingernut and Raspberry Puddings

200ml cream, whipped until firm
100ml mascarpone
2 tablespoons icing sugar
200g fresh raspberries
1¹/₄ cups sweet sherry or green ginger wine
2 x 250g packets gingernut biscuits
extra 100ml cream, lightly whipped, for serving
extra fresh raspberries for serving
extra icing sugar to decorate

Combine the whipped cream, mascarpone and icing sugar. Lightly mash the raspberries. Fold the raspberries through the whipped cream mixture. Pour the sherry into a shallow dish.

Assemble each pudding as you go. One at a time, dunk each biscuit into the sherry or green ginger wine and completely submerge it for 10 seconds. Lay one biscuit down, spoon a tablespoon of filling over and place another dunked gingernut biscuit on top. Continue this process until all the biscuits and filling are used. Refrigerate the puddings for 1 hour before serving.

Place each pudding on a serving plate and top with a dollop of whipped cream, some fresh raspberries and a shake of icing sugar.

MAKES 20

Gingernut and Raspberry Puddings

warm up

A nourishing breakfast of creamy mushrooms and prosciutto on toast. Satisfying soups made with your best stock. Crusty pies filled with salmon or lamb. Rich desserts of smooth shiny chocolate, aromatic ginger or sweet pot-roasted quince to revive the tired body. Melt away the wintry chill and warm up the body before returning to enjoy the crispness and clarity of the day once more.

Curried Parsnip and Pear Soup

2 tablespoons butter
1 onion, peeled and coarsely chopped
1 clove garlic, peeled and sliced
1 teaspoon ground cumin
1 teaspoon ground coriander
$^1/_2$ teaspoon ground turmeric
sea salt and freshly ground black pepper to taste
4 cups peeled, chopped parsnips
2 large pears, peeled, cored and diced
$1^1/_2$ litres chicken stock
100ml cream
Fried Croutons (see page 10) to garnish
fresh coriander sprigs to garnish

Melt the butter in a heavy-bottomed saucepan. Fry the onion and garlic over a low heat until soft. Stir in the cumin, coriander, turmeric, salt and pepper. Cook for 2 minutes. Add the parsnips, pears and chicken stock. Cook, covered, until the parsnips are tender. Allow to cool, then purée. Return to the saucepan and reheat. Stir the cream in and serve piping hot, garnished with Fried Croutons and fresh coriander.

SERVES 6

Bluff Oyster Soup

For Bluff oyster-lovers – the oysters are barely cooked but full of that classic flavour.

1 small leek
2 tablespoons butter
2 tablespoons plain flour
400ml fish stock
$^1/_4$ cup oyster juice (drained from the oysters)
24 bluff oysters, drained of juice
100ml milk
200ml cream
sea salt and freshly ground black pepper to taste
1 teaspoon grated lemon zest
2 tablespoons lemon juice
chopped fresh chives to garnish

Halve the leek lengthways and slice thinly. Gently fry the leek in the butter in a saucepan until softened. Stir in the flour to make a paste. Add the fish stock and stir until the mixture thickens. Add the oyster juice and gently simmer the soup with the lid on for 10 minutes. Finely chop half the oysters. Remove the soup from the heat and stir in the milk and cream, salt and pepper to taste, lemon zest, lemon juice and the chopped oysters. Reheat the soup over a low heat. When ready to serve, drop in the remaining dozen oysters and warm them through. Serve immediately, finished with chopped chives.

SERVES 4–6

Bluff Oyster Soup

Roast Tomato, Pepper and Basil Soup

Before, during or after sports, hot soup is delicious and warming.

8 large tomatoes, halved
4 cloves garlic, peeled
sea salt and freshly ground black pepper
1 teaspoon sugar
4 red peppers (capsicums), roasted and skinned
   see below
1 teaspoon butter
1 cup fresh basil leaves
4 cups vegetable stock
a few basil leaves to garnish
cracked black pepper to garnish
sea salt to garnish

Place the tomatoes flesh-side up with the garlic in a roasting pan, season with salt and pepper and sprinkle with sugar. Roast in an oven preheated to 190°C for 30–40 minutes or until soft. Place the tomatoes, garlic, peppers, butter and basil leaves in a food processor with 1 cup of vegetable stock and process until smooth. Put the mixture into a saucepan with the remaining stock and heat until hot. Serve garnished with basil leaves, cracked black pepper, sea salt and accompanied by warm crusty bread.

SERVES 6

Roasting and Skinning Peppers

Use an electric grill or the oven. Halve the peppers and remove the seeds and white ribs. Oil the peppers, place them cut side down on aluminium foil on a baking tray and grill or roast until the skin blackens. Place the peppers in a plastic bag or cover with a cloth for 15 minutes. When they are cool enough to handle peel off the skins.

Bean and Sausage Soup

250g borlotti or dried white beans, soaked
   overnight in cold water
2 tablespoons olive oil
1 clove garlic, peeled and finely chopped
1 small onion, peeled and finely chopped
1 stalk celery, finely sliced
2 cups butternut pumpkin, finely diced
1 large potato, peeled and finely diced
$1/2$ cup orzo pasta
3 chorizo sausages, finely sliced
1 cup fresh basil leaves
sea salt and ground black pepper to taste
400g can chopped tomatoes in juice
600ml beef stock
fresh flat-leaf parsley or basil leaves to garnish

Drain the beans and dry on kitchen paper. Heat the olive oil and sauté the beans, garlic and onion in a large saucepan over a gentle heat until the onion softens. Add the celery, butternut, potato, orzo, sausages and fresh basil. Sauté the ingredients for 5 minutes, then season to taste with salt and pepper. Add the tomatoes and beef stock. Cover and gently simmer until the beans and pasta are tender. Garnish with parsley or basil leaves. Serve with crusty bread.

SERVES 6

Red Pepper and Pistachio Salsa

A hardy store-cupboard salsa to have on hand.
Serve on a favourite bread with drinks or on the side
with grilled fish and chicken for a warming tang.

2 tablespoons olive oil
6 spring onions, trimmed and chopped
2 cloves garlic, peeled and chopped
2 red peppers (capsicums), deseeded and sliced
1 teaspoon ground cumin
1 teaspoon ground coriander
1 teaspoon smoked paprika
2 tablespoons sweet chilli sauce
1 tablespoon tomato paste
1/4 cup lemon juice
sea salt and freshly ground black pepper to taste
1/4 cup fresh mint leaves
1 cup pistachio nuts
6 tablespoons avocado oil
1 tablespoon balsamic vinegar

Put the olive oil in a frying pan and fry the spring onions, garlic and red peppers together over a gentle heat until soft. Stir in the cumin, coriander, paprika, chilli sauce, tomato paste, lemon juice and salt and pepper. Cook for 10 minutes over a gentle heat. Place the mint leaves and pistachio nuts in a food processor and pulse until coarsely chopped. Add the pepper mixture, avocado oil and balsamic vinegar and blend together to a chunky salsa.

MAKES 5 CUPS

Fast Flat Bread

15g (2 tablespoons) fresh yeast
15g (1 tablespoon) sugar
310ml tepid water
500g (4 cups) plain flour
15g (1 tablespoon) salt

Dissolve the yeast and sugar in half the tepid water. Place the flour and salt in a bowl. Make a well in the centre and pour in the dissolved yeast. Using your fingers or a fork, stir the flour into the yeast mixture until the liquid has soaked into the flour. Add the remaining tepid water and gradually combine to form a moist dough. Place the dough on a lightly floured surface and knead the dough vigorously for 5 minutes. Dust your hands with a little flour if the dough sticks. Place the dough in a clean bowl, dust the top with flour, cover with plastic food wrap and leave in a warm place to prove and double in size (30–40 minutes).

Knock down the dough. Divide the dough into 18 even balls and roll each ball flat in a rough circle to about 2–3cm thick. For flat bread, prick the dough all over with a fork. If you prefer puffy bread, don't prick it. Bake the bread on the bars of the oven racks in an oven preheated to 220°C for 4–5 minutes.

Red Pepper and Pistachio Salsa

Pan-fried Duck Breast with Onion, Orange and Raisin Sauce

6 duck breasts
$1/2$ cup fresh orange juice
3 bay leaves
sea salt and freshly ground black pepper to taste
$1/2$ cup raisins
1 large white onion, peeled, halved and thinly sliced
$1/4$ cup olive oil
1 tablespoon butter
2 tablespoons white wine vinegar
extra $1/4$ cup fresh orange juice
$1/2$ cup chicken, veal or duck stock
flour
2 tablespoons olive oil
2 tablespoons pine nuts
2 tablespoons finely chopped fresh flat-leaf parsley
1 tablespoon red currant jelly

Using a sharp knife, score the skin and surface of each duck breast. Place the breasts skin-side down in the orange juice with the bay leaves, salt and pepper. Marinate for an hour. Soak the raisins in lukewarm water while you prepare the onion.

Place the onion, olive oil and butter in a small frying pan and fry over a low heat until the onion softens. Add the white wine vinegar, second measure of orange juice and stock, and simmer for 10 minutes.

When ready to cook the breasts, remove them from the orange marinade, reserving the liquid, and dry on kitchen paper. Dust the breasts with a little flour. Heat the olive oil in a large heavy-bottomed frying pan over a medium heat. Fry the breasts skin-side down for about 4–5 minutes each side with a knob of butter. Place in an oven preheated to 180°C for 5 minutes or until just cooked through. Set aside and keep warm for 5 minutes while you finish the sauce.

Drain the raisins. Pour the onion and orange mixture into the pan you cooked the breasts in. Add the marinade from the duck breasts, raisins, pine nuts, parsley and red currant jelly. Simmer the sauce rapidly over a medium to high heat for 5 minutes. Slice the duck breasts and arrange on a serving plate. Spoon the sauce over the duck and serve with Wilted Winter Greens (see below).

SERVES 6

Wilted Winter Greens

Allow 2 cups of packed greens per person.

any combination of greens, such as spinach, silverbeet (stalks removed), rocket, watercress, shanghai cabbage
2–3 cloves of garlic, peeled and grated
2 tablespoons olive oil
2 tablespoons butter
sea salt and cracked black pepper
lemon juice

Wash and trim any coarse stalks from the greens, drain and dry on kitchen paper. Gently fry the garlic in a heavy-bottomed frying pan in a little olive oil and knob of butter until soft. Increase the heat and begin dropping in the greens. With the pan hot enough so that any moisture from the greens evaporates quickly, toss until the greens begin to wilt. Season to taste with salt, pepper and a squeeze of lemon juice. Serve the greens at room temperature.

SERVES 6

Pan-fried Duck Breast with Onion, Orange and Raisin Sauce

Chilli Con Carne

Aromatic and quick to ladle into bowls and warm up the tribe. For a more substantial meal, serve with rice and warm tortillas on the side.

2 tablespoons olive oil
1 large onion, finely chopped
2 cloves garlic, peeled and grated
2 small fresh red 'birds eye' chillies, deseeded and finely chopped
1 teaspoon ground cumin
500g prime minced beef
2 tablespoons tomato paste
400g can tomatoes in juice, chopped
1/2 cup tomato sauce
420g can chillied red kidney beans
200ml water
sour cream to garnish
fresh coriander to garnish

Heat the oil over a medium heat in a heavy-bottomed saucepan. Add the onion and garlic and fry until soft. Add the chopped red chillies, cumin and minced beef. Break up the meat and continue to cook, stirring, until meat is brown. Add the tomato paste, tomatoes in juice, tomato sauce, kidney beans and water. Cover and simmer over a low heat for 45 minutes to 1 hour until the chilli is thick. Finish with a dollop of sour cream and fresh coriander on top.

SERVES 6

Spinach and Chickpea Stew with Grilled Sausages and Mash

425g can chickpeas
baby spinach leaves, enough for 6
$^1/_4$ cup olive oil
1 red onion, finely chopped
2 cloves garlic, peeled and grated
2 stalks celery, thinly sliced
sea salt and freshly ground black pepper
pinch of sugar
pinch of ground nutmeg or to taste
pinch of ground cumin or to taste
400g can peeled tomatoes in juice, chopped
$^1/_2$ cup tomato purée
2 tablespoons lemon juice
12 favourite sausages, grilled until cooked
Chive Mash (see below)

Drain the chickpeas and set aside. Wash, drain and dry the spinach. Heat the olive oil in a saucepan over a low heat and fry the onion, garlic and celery until soft. Season with salt, pepper, sugar and spices. Add the chickpeas, tomatoes, tomato purée and lemon juice. Cover and simmer rapidly for 10 minutes. Remove the lid and simmer for a further 5 minutes or until the sauce begins to thicken. Drop in the spinach and stir together until the spinach wilts.

Place two grilled sausages on each plate, spoon the Spinach and Chickpea Stew over them and a scoop of Chive Mash on the side.

SERVES 6

Chive Mash

6 large floury potatoes, peeled
salt
butter to taste
cream and/or milk
sea salt and freshly ground black pepper to taste
$^1/_4$ cup finely chopped chives

Place the potatoes in a saucepan with enough water to cover and season with salt. Cover and simmer until the potatoes are tender. Drain. Add butter and mash with enough cream and/or milk to achieve a smooth, thick creamy consistency. Season with salt and pepper and stir in the chives.

SERVES 6

Spinach and Chickpea Stew with Grilled Sausages
and Mash

Lamb and Kumara Pie

The stock needs to settle overnight in the refrigerator, so make it the day before.

PIE FILLING STEP ONE
4 lamb shanks, trimmed of fat
plain flour
2–3 tablespoons olive oil
1 onion, peeled and quartered
2 carrots, coarsely chopped
2 stalks celery
6 peppercorns
2 bay leaves
3 tablespoons tomato paste
$1^{1}/_{2}$ cups red wine
4 cups veal or beef stock

PIE FILLING STEP TWO
stock prepared in Step One
50g butter
1 onion, peeled and finely chopped
1 clove garlic, peeled and grated
6 tablespoons plain flour
2 tablespoons fresh rosemary
$^{1}/_{4}$ cup finely chopped fresh flat-leaf parsley
$1^{1}/_{2}$ cups peeled, cooked and diced golden
  kumara (sweet potato)
sea salt and freshly ground black pepper to taste

PASTRY
2 cups plain flour
125g cold butter, cubed
pinch of salt
1 egg
about 1 tablespoon cold water
1 egg, beaten, for sealing and glazing

STEP ONE
To make the filling, dust each lamb shank with a little flour. Heat the oil in a heavy-bottomed saucepan over a medium heat. Brown the lamb shanks two at a time. Place the remaining ingredients and the browned shanks in the saucepan and gently simmer with the lid on for about 2 hours until the meat begins to fall from the bone. Remove the shanks and set aside to cool. Refrigerate. Strain the vegetables from the stock and discard them. Allow the stock to cool, then refrigerate it overnight to allow time for the fat to rise and set on the surface.

STEP TWO
Next day remove the fat from the stock with a spoon. You should have about $3^{1}/_{4}$ cups of jellied stock. Simmer the stock for about 10 minutes to reduce it to $2^{1}/_{4}$ cups of liquid stock. Cut the meat from the shanks and slice it into bite-sized pieces.

Melt the butter in a saucepan and gently fry the onion and garlic until soft. Stir in the flour to make a roux. Using a whisk stir in the stock and continue to stir until you have a smooth sauce. Add the rosemary, parsley, kumara, salt and pepper and sliced lamb shanks. Allow the filling to cool.

PASTRY AND ASSEMBLY
To make the pastry, place the flour, butter and salt in a food processor and process until the mixture resembles fine breadcrumbs. Add the egg and continue to process, adding enough of the cold water to bind the dough together. Remove the mixture to a lightly floured board and form the dough into a ball. Wrap in plastic food wrap and refrigerate for 20 minutes.

To assemble the pie, grease a 23cm pie plate with butter. On a lightly floured board roll out the pastry large enough to line the pie plate plus extra to fold over and cover the pie. Allow the excess dough to flop over the edge of the pie plate. Spoon the cooled pie filling into the pastry. Fold the excess pastry over the pie. Patch the top as required and seal with a little beaten egg. Brush the top of the pie with the remaining beaten egg. Bake in an oven preheated to 190°C for 40–45 minutes until cooked and golden.

SERVES 6

Lamb and Kumara Pie

Salmon Pie

Salmon Pie

A soft, sensual pie to satisfy the soul.

400g fresh salmon fillet, skin on
2 tablespoons butter
1 small leek, thinly sliced
100g butter
$^1/_4$ cup plain flour
$1^1/_4$ cups milk
grated zest of 1 lemon
$^1/_4$ cup lemon juice
sea salt and freshly ground black pepper to taste
$^1/_2$ cup chopped fresh chives, dill or flat-leaf parsley
400g store-bought puff pastry
4 eggs, hard-boiled, peeled and coarsely chopped
1 egg, lightly beaten, for glazing

Lightly poach the salmon by placing it in a shallow frying pan, skin down, with enough water to cover the flesh. Bring the water to boiling point and then turn down the heat so that the water just shivers. Cook for 4–5 minutes or until the salmon is still slightly underdone. Remove from the pan and allow to cool.

Melt the 2 tablespoons of butter in a frying pan and gently fry the leeks until they soften, then set aside. Melt the 100g of butter in a saucepan, stir in the flour and gently cook for a minute over a medium heat. Add a third of the milk and stir the sauce with a whisk until it fully thickens. Add the remaining milk and continue to stir the sauce to a thick, smooth finish. Remove from the heat and stir in the lemon zest, juice, salt and pepper, chives and leeks. While this cools, butter a 18–20cm oval or round pie dish. Divide the pastry in half. Roll out each half on a lightly floured board large enough to cut an 18–20cm shape from each half. Place one half of the pastry in the bottom of the pie dish. Spoon the white sauce over the pastry, leaving a 5cm margin around the edge. Sprinkle the chopped egg over. Break the salmon into chunks, removing the skin and pin bones as you go. Place the salmon evenly over the egg. Dampen the uncovered margin around the filling with a little beaten egg. Place over the other pastry half and gently ease it into place to completely cover the filling. Fold the bottom edge over the top edge of pastry. Seal and flatten the edge with a fork or your fingers. Chill the pie in the fridge for 20 minutes.

Brush the top of the pie with the remaining beaten egg. Score the pie top in a random crisscross pattern without piercing the pastry through to the filling. Bake in an oven preheated to 215–220°C for 30–40 minutes until the pie is golden brown and crisp.

SERVES 6

Mozzarella and Ham Fried Sandwich

A twist on the classic French Croque Monsieur, this is guaranteed to satisfy hungry appetites.

12 slices Italian-style bread
Dijon mustard
400g fresh mozzarella cheese, thinly sliced
12 thin slices ham
100ml extra virgin olive oil

Lay six slices of bread on a flat surface. Spread each slice with a thin layer of Dijon mustard. Divide the mozzarella evenly between the slices of bread, placing the cheese slices flat on the bread. Top the cheese with a slice of ham and a second slice of bread. Heat a little oil in a non-stick pan over a moderate heat and fry the sandwiches in batches until golden on each side and the cheese starts to ooze. Add extra oil as needed. Alternatively, use a sandwich press. Brush both sides of the sandwich with olive oil and cook until golden.

MAKES 6

Mozzarella and Ham Fried Sandwich

Corned Beef, Swede Mash and Mustard Parsley Sauce

Warm and refuel the body with this old-fashioned favourite.

2–2.5kg corned silverside, washed
4 whole cloves
water to cover
2 bay leaves
6 peppercorns
$1/4$ cup brown sugar
2 onions, peeled and quartered
$1/4$ cup malt vinegar
12 small red-skinned potatoes, washed
6 medium carrots, peeled
about 3 small leeks, washed, trimmed and cut
   into thirds
Swede Mash (see below)
Mustard Parsley Sauce (see below)

Stud the silverside with the whole cloves and place in a large heavy-bottomed saucepan. Cover with water. Add the bay leaves. Cover with a lid and simmer for 1 hour. Taste the water. If it's too salty, tip out half the cooking liquid, replace it with fresh water and return to the heat. Add the peppercorns, brown sugar, onions and malt vinegar, cover and simmer a further hour. Test the corned beef for tenderness. When you estimate it will take another 30 minutes to cook, begin to add the vegetables to be cooked with the meat. First add the potatoes and simmer for 10 minutes. Add the carrots. Ten minutes later add the leeks. After another 10 minutes the meat and vegetables should all be cooked. Drain and reserve $1/4$ cup of cooking liquid for the Mustard Parsley Sauce.

   Serve the corned beef and vegetables with Swede Mash. Spoon Mustard Parsley Sauce over the top.

SERVES 6

Swede Mash

3 medium swedes, peeled and quartered
butter
sea salt and freshly ground black pepper
pinch of nutmeg

Steam the swedes until very tender. Mash with enough butter to achieve a smooth, creamy mash. Season to taste with salt, plenty of pepper and the nutmeg.

SERVES 6

Mustard Parsley Sauce

75g butter
$1^1/2$ tablespoons plain flour
1 teaspoon Dijon mustard
$1^1/4$ cups milk, warmed
$1/4$ cup liquid from the corned beef
freshly ground pepper to taste
$1/2$ cup finely chopped fresh flat-leaf parsley

Melt the butter in a saucepan over a low to medium heat. Stir in the flour and mustard. Pour the warmed milk in and stir continuously with a whisk until the sauce is smooth and thickened. Stir in the corned beef liquid, pepper to taste and parsley.

MAKES ABOUT 2 CUPS

Mushrooms on Toast

A replenishing breakfast or late brunch.

1 small clove garlic, peeled and grated
50g butter
1 tablespoon olive oil
600g dark flat mushrooms, whole, halved, quartered or sliced
sea salt and freshly ground black pepper
1 teaspoon Dijon mustard
1 tablespoon plain flour
1–1$\frac{1}{4}$ cups cream or milk
$\frac{1}{4}$ cup chopped fresh flat-leaf parsley
1–2 tablespoons lemon juice
6 generous slices rustic country bread, toasted or grilled
12 rashers streaky bacon, prosciutto or pancetta, grilled until crisp

Soften the garlic in the butter and olive oil in a large frying pan over a low to medium heat. Add the mushrooms, salt and pepper and gently fry until tender. Stir in the mustard and the flour and coat the mushrooms. Pour the cream or milk in and constantly stir the mushrooms until the sauce thickens. Add the parsley and lemon juice to taste. Spoon the mushrooms onto the toast and serve with grilled bacon, prosciutto or pancetta.

SERVES 6

Mushrooms on Toast

Black Magic Pudding with Chocolate Sauce

Sure to appease chocoholics' cravings.

1 tablespoon butter, melted
100g dark cooking chocolate
6 large eggs, separated
$^1/_2$ cup caster sugar
1 tablespoon dark rum
$^1/_4$ cup ground hazelnuts
$^1/_4$ cup fine fresh breadcrumbs

Preheat the oven to 180°C. Brush a 1-litre pudding bowl with melted butter. Break up the chocolate and melt in a double boiler or on a low heat in the microwave and allow to cool. Whisk the egg yolks and half the sugar together until thick and foamy. Stir in the rum and chocolate. Beat the egg whites until stiff and gradually beat in the remaining sugar. Fold the egg white mixture, hazelnuts and breadcrumbs into the chocolate mixture. Pour the mixture into the pudding bowl and loosely cover with aluminium foil. Bake in a bain-marie for about 1 hour until just set. Allow to cool for 10 minutes before inverting onto a serving plate. Serve drizzled with a little Chocolate Sauce (see page 37).

SERVES 6

Apple, Chocolate and Nut Cake

With fruity, moist cakes like this a skewer test will not always indicate when the cake is cooked. It is ready when the top is firm and the cake comes away from the sides of the tin.

200g butter, softened
200g (1 cup) caster sugar
4 large eggs
pinch of salt
225g (1$^3/_4$ cups) plain flour, sifted
1$^1/_2$ teaspoons baking powder, sifted
200g dark chocolate, coarsely chopped
2 apples, peeled, cored and cut into small dice
1 cup pistachio nuts
1 tablespoon grated lemon zest

Preheat the oven to 180°C. Cream the butter and sugar in a bowl until pale and fluffy. Beat in the eggs one at a time. Stir in the salt, flour and baking powder until well combined. Stir in the chocolate, apples, nuts and lemon zest. Pour into a lightly buttered 22cm loose-bottomed cake tin. Bake for 1 hour. Allow to cool in the tin for 5 minutes then turn out onto a wire cooling rack. Serve the cake warm while the chocolate is still soft, with lashings of lightly whipped cream. If the cake cools before you serve it, simply warm portions in the microwave.

SERVES 10

Ginger Cake with Lemon Syrup, Poached Pears and Custard Cream

125g butter, softened
200g (1 cup) brown sugar
2 small eggs
1 tablespoon honey
1 tablespoon golden syrup
1/4 cup lemon juice
180g (1 1/2 cups) plain flour, sifted
2 teaspoons baking powder, sifted
2 teaspoons powdered ginger

LEMON SYRUP
1/2 cup lemon juice
1/2 cup caster sugar

Poached Pears (see below)
Custard Cream (see below)

Preheat the oven to 175°C. Cream the butter and sugar in a bowl until thick and creamy. Beat in the eggs one at a time. Add the honey, golden syrup and lemon juice. Mix together the flour, baking powder and ginger. Stir the dry ingredients into the creamed ingredients. Pour into a buttered and floured 18cm Bundt tin or buttered 20cm loose-bottomed cake tin and bake for 30–35 minutes or until a skewer comes out clean. Remove from the pan and allow to cool on a wire rack for 10 minutes.

To make the Lemon Syrup, stir the lemon juice and caster sugar together in a small saucepan over a low heat until the sugar dissolves.

Transfer the cake to a serving plate and pour the syrup over while the cake is still warm, allowing the syrup to soak in. Serve a slice of Ginger Cake alongside Poached Pears drizzled with a little Custard Cream.

SERVES 6

Poached Pears

2 cups caster sugar
1 cup water
50ml sweet dessert white wine
squeeze of lemon juice
6 medium-sized sweet pears, peeled and
    left whole

Combine the caster sugar, water, white wine and lemon juice in a saucepan and stir over a low heat until the sugar dissolves. Place the pears in the syrup and cover with a lid. Gently poach the pears until they become tender, about 30 minutes. Remove the pears from the syrup and place in a serving dish. Simmer the syrup for 5 more minutes with the lid off to reduce it, then pour it over the pears.

SERVES 6

Custard Cream

1 1/2 cups milk
1/2 cup cream
6 egg yolks
1/2 cup Vanilla Sugar (see page 99)

Heat the milk and cream to boiling point in a saucepan, then remove from the heat. While the milk and cream are heating, whisk the egg yolks and Vanilla Sugar together in a bowl until thick and pale. Gradually whisk the hot liquid into the egg yolks and sugar. Return the custard to the saucepan and continuously stir over a low heat until the custard thickens and coats the back of the spoon.

MAKES 2 1/2 CUPS

Baked Tamarillos

8 firm, ripe tamarillos
6 tablespoons Vanilla Sugar (see below)
$^1/_4$ cup brandy

Remove the stalks from the tamarillos. To skin the tamarillos, blanch them in boiling water for 30 seconds, then plunge into cold water and peel off the skin. Vertically halve the fruit and place them cut side up in a baking dish. Sprinkle the fruit with Vanilla Sugar to taste, and a couple of sploshes of brandy. Bake the tamarillos in an oven preheated to about 230°C for about 5 minutes until the fruit is tender. Serve with Coffee Crème Brûlée (see page 100).

SERVES 8

Vanilla Sugar

2 fresh, moist vanilla pods
500g caster sugar

Cut the vanilla pods into small pieces. Place the pods and sugar in a food processor and pulse together until the sugar is ash-coloured. Sieve the mixture, return the lumps to the food processor, pulse again and add them to the rest of the sugar. Store in an airtight container.

MAKES ABOUT 2$^1/_4$ CUPS

Pot-roasted Quince

8 small quinces, unpeeled
3¹/₂ cups caster sugar
¹/₂ cup liquid honey
1¹/₄ litres water
2 bay leaves
cream for serving

Thoroughly wash the velvet from the quinces but do not peel them. Place the quinces in a large saucepan in a single tight-fitting layer. Sprinkle the sugar over them. Drizzle the honey over and add the water. Slowly bring the quinces and liquid to a gentle simmer, making sure the sugar dissolves before boiling point is reached. Add the bay leaves. Cover the saucepan with a loose-fitting lid and simmer very gently for 1 hour. Carefully turn the quinces. Remove the bay leaves and continue to gently simmer with the lid on for a further 3 hours until the quinces are pink and tender, turning every hour. Allow to cool. Serve warm with cream.

SERVES 8

Coffee Crème Brûlée

8 egg yolks
4 tablespoons caster sugar
600ml cream
1 cup strong brewed espresso coffee
2 tablespoons brown sugar, sifted
2 tablespoons icing sugar, sifted

Whisk the egg yolks and caster sugar together in a bowl until pale and thick. Place the cream and coffee in a heavy-bottomed saucepan and heat to boiling point. Remove from the heat and whisk in the egg and sugar mixture. Return to a low heat and stir continuously until the custard thickens enough to coat the back of a spoon. Strain the custard into a jug. Pour the custard into eight 150ml ramekins. Place the ramekins in a baking pan and fill the baking pan with water to halfway up the sides of the ramekins.

Bake in an oven preheated to 140°C for about 40 minutes until the custard is just set. Remove the ramekins from the pan. Allow to cool and refrigerate until chilled. At least 2 hours before serving, combine the sifted sugars and sprinkle the mixture evenly over the surface of the custards.

Place the ramekins under a hot grill, close to the heat, and cook until the sugar is golden and caramelised. Allow to cool and return to the fridge to chill. Serve with Baked Tamarillos (see page 99) on the side.

SERVES 8

Pot-roasted Quince

Bananas with Ice Cream and
Caramel Sauce

Bananas with Ice Cream and Caramel Sauce

Easy to whip up for unexpected arrivals.

12 ice cream wafers
6 small bananas, peeled and split
$^1/_2$ litre favourite ice cream
200ml cream, whipped until thick
Caramel Sauce (see below)

For each serving lay a wafer on the serving plate and top with a split banana, ice cream and a drizzle of Caramel Sauce. Top with another wafer then more ice cream, cream and additional Caramel Sauce.

SERVES 6

Caramel Sauce

$1^1/_4$ cups sugar
100ml water
150ml cream

Dissolve the sugar in the water in a heavy-bottomed saucepan over a low heat, stirring occasionally. Bring to a gentle steady simmer and allow the syrup to caramelise to a dark golden colour. While it caramelises, warm the cream. Remove the caramelised sugar from the heat and stir in the warm cream until the sauce is smooth.

MAKES ABOUT $1^1/_4$ CUPS

time out

Take time out to bring in and cook the catch – a sweet seafood broth, a trout enveloped in streaky bacon, wood-roasted salmon cakes. Time out a for revitalising swim and a beach banquet of silverbeet and pecorino tart, and piquant chicken, avocado and fennel salad. Time out for golf and sweet treats of feijoa jam pikelets after the round. Or take time out simply to lie under the trees and feel replete.

Seafood and Vegetable Broth

Take time to prepare and linger over this hands-on meal. Share it with friends and savour the seafood juices.

$^1/_4$ cup extra virgin olive oil
1 small leek, washed, trimmed and thinly sliced
2 cloves garlic, peeled and grated
1 rasher streaky bacon, finely chopped
1 fresh red chilli, deseeded and finely chopped
1 tablespoon grated lemon zest
1 cup peeled, diced potato
2 x 400g cans Italian tomatoes in juice, puréed
4 ripe tomatoes, finely chopped
1 tablespoon tomato paste
1 cup white wine
1$^1/_2$ cups fish stock
$^1/_2$ cup chopped fresh flat-leaf parsley
$^1/_2$ cup chopped marjoram leaves
sea salt and freshly ground black pepper to taste
2 tablespoons lemon juice

150g firm-fleshed, skinned white fish (cod, hapuku, hoki), cut into
   bite-sized pieces
12 small mussels
12 southern clams
12 scallops
crusty bread for serving

Heat the oil in a large saucepan over a medium heat. Add the leek and garlic and cook until soft. Add the bacon and cook for 5 minutes. Add the chilli, lemon zest, potato, canned and fresh tomatoes, tomato paste, wine, fish stock, parsley, marjoram, salt and pepper and lemon juice. Reduce to a low heat and gently simmer, covered, for 20 minutes.

   When ready to serve, drop in the fish, mussels and clams. Cover and simmer for about 4 minutes or until the shellfish open. Discard any unopened shellfish. Drop in the scallops and cook for a further 1 minute. Serve immediately with crusty bread.

SERVES 6

Seafood and Vegetable Broth

Braised Lamb Shanks

Once this is in the oven, the long, slow cooking enables you to take time out for some outdoor pleasures.

6 lamb shanks
sea salt and freshly ground black pepper
plain flour
olive oil
2 rashers streaky bacon, diced
2 red onions, peeled and quartered
3 cloves garlic, peeled and sliced
4 sprigs fresh rosemary
2 bay leaves
4 large potatoes, peeled and cut into chunks
6 carrots, peeled and halved
3 parsnips, peeled and halved
2 golden kumara, peeled and cut into chunks
1 bottle white wine
water

Season the lamb shanks with salt and pepper and lightly flour each shank. In a heavy-bottomed frying pan or casserole dish brown each lamb shank over a medium heat using a little olive oil. Place the browned lamb shanks in a large casserole dish or high-sided baking dish. Scatter the bacon, onions, garlic, rosemary, bay leaves and vegetables over the shanks. Pour in the white wine and enough water to just cover the ingredients. Cover with aluminium foil and seal. Bake in an oven preheated to 175°C for about 4 hours until the meat is easily pulled away from the bone. Serve one shank per person, accompanied with the vegetables and sauce.

SERVES 6

Pikelets

Enjoy these topped with feijoa jam and cream in the late summer sun on a lazy day.

1 cup self-raising flour
$^1/_4$ teaspoon baking soda
3 tablespoons caster sugar
1 egg, beaten
$^3/_4$ cup milk
1 tablespoon butter, melted
butter for cooking

Sift the flour and baking soda into a bowl. Make a well in the centre and add the sugar, egg, milk and melted butter. Stir the mixture from the centre, drawing in the dry ingredients until you have a smooth batter. Heat a heavy-bottomed frying pan to a medium heat. Grease with a little butter. Drop tablespoonfuls of batter into the pan in batches. Cook until bubbles burst and break the surface of the pikelet and the underside is golden brown. Turn and brown the other side.

MAKES 18–20

Fast Feijoa Jam

1kg firm, ripe feijoas, peeled and coarsely sliced
$^1/_4$ cup water
4 cups sugar
2 tablespoons lemon juice
grated zest of 1 lemon

Place the feijoas and water in a saucepan and simmer for 10 minutes until soft. Add the sugar, lemon juice and lemon zest. Stir until the sugar dissolves and return to a steady simmer. Cook for a further 10 minutes until the mixture gels when tested (see page 132). Remove from the heat. Pour into clean, warm sterilised jars and seal.

MAKES 8 CUPS

Pikelets

Fettuccine with Broccolini and Walnuts

A quick, energising lunch for after a morning dip.

600g fettuccine
300g broccolini, blanched
2 cloves garlic, peeled and grated
1 onion, peeled and finely chopped
2 tablespoons olive oil
sea salt and freshly ground black pepper to taste
$^1/_2$ cup finely chopped walnuts
$^1/_2$ cup finely chopped fresh flat-leaf parsley
$^1/_2$ cup parmesan cheese, grated
extra virgin olive oil
feta cheese (optional)

Cook the fettuccine in a large saucepan of salted boiling water until al dente.

Meanwhile, chop the blanched broccolini quite finely and set aside. Fry the garlic and onion in the olive oil in a frying pan over a gentle heat until soft. Season with salt and pepper and add the broccolini, walnuts, parsley and cooked, drained fettuccine. Stir and heat through. Toss the parmesan through and transfer to a serving bowl. Drizzle and toss with a little extra virgin olive oil to moisten.

This is also delicious sprinkled with a little crumbled feta cheese.

SERVES 4

Roast Sage Pork

2kg piece belly pork, skin thinly scored in a
 crisscross pattern
1^1/$_2$ cups fresh sage leaves
1 tablespoon fresh grated ginger
2 tablespoons sea salt
2 tablespoons lemon juice
1 tablespoon honey
extra virgin olive oil
1 tablespoon balsamic vinegar

Lay the scored pork in a baking pan. Place the sage leaves, ginger, salt, lemon juice and honey in a food processor. Pulse to pulp. Drizzle in enough olive oil to create a thick paste. Massage the paste into the skin of the pork and leave to marinate for 2 hours or overnight.

When ready to cook, moisten the bottom of the baking pan with olive oil and balsamic vinegar. Roast the pork in an oven preheated to 180°C for 1^1/$_2$ hours, occasionally basting the meat. Increase the oven temperature to 200°C and continue to cook the meat a further 30 minutes. If the surface of the pork is not crackly enough, place the pork under a hot grill for 5–10 minutes to finish it off. Allow the meat to stand for 10 minutes before carving.

SERVES 6

Silverbeet and Pecorino Tart

750g silverbeet
1 onion, peeled and finely chopped
1 clove garlic, peeled and grated
1 tablespoon olive oil
4 canned anchovy fillets, mashed (optional)
^{3}/$_4$ cup grated pecorino cheese
sea salt and freshly ground black pepper to taste
6 eggs, beaten
^{1}/$_2$ cup cream
4 sheets filo pastry
2 tablespoons butter, melted

Shred the silverbeet leaves and stems finely. Place the silverbeet in a large saucepan with 3 cups of water and a dash of salt. Simmer for 5 minutes, then drain and cool. Squeeze out any excess water and dry on kitchen paper. Fry the onion and garlic in a frying pan in the olive oil over a gentle heat until soft. Add the silverbeet and gently cook for a further 10 minutes. Transfer to a bowl and add the anchovies (if liked), pecorino and salt and pepper and combine. Stir in the beaten eggs and cream.

Butter a 22cm ceramic pie dish. Line the pie dish with a sheet of pastry and brush lightly with melted butter. Place another sheet across at an angle then repeat the process with the melted butter and remaining pastry sheets to evenly line the pie dish. Spoon the filling in. Bake in an oven preheated to 170°C for 20–30 minutes until just set. Serve the tart warm.

SERVES 6

Cheese Soufflé

Light and tasty served with a crisp green salad after a walk in the woods or a quick round of golf.

3 tablespoons butter
3$^1/_2$ tablespoons plain flour
1$^1/_4$ cups milk
1 teaspoon Dijon mustard
60g pecorino cheese, grated
60g tasty cheese, grated
sea salt and freshly ground black pepper to taste
4 eggs, separated

Preheat the oven to 190°C and butter a 1.5-litre soufflé dish. Melt the butter in a saucepan and stir the flour in. Over a medium heat stir in the milk with a whisk and continue stirring to achieve a smooth, thick sauce. Stir in the mustard and cheese and season with salt and pepper. Stir until the cheese has just melted. Remove from the heat and allow to cool slightly. Stir in the egg yolks one at a time. Beat the egg whites until they are stiff. Fold the egg whites into the cheese mixture. Spoon into the prepared soufflé dish and bake for 25–30 minutes.

SERVES 4

Cheese Soufflé

Trout Wrapped in Streaky Bacon

Traditional but tasty treatment for the day's catch.
Delicious served with creamy Grated Potato
Dauphinoise.

STUFFING
1 small leek, trimmed of green leaves and
   finely sliced
2 tablespoons butter
1 rasher bacon, finely chopped
2 cups fresh breadcrumbs
1 tablespoon finely chopped parsley
1 tablespoon finely chopped fresh dill
1 tablespoon grated lemon zest
2 tablespoons lemon juice
sea salt and freshly ground black pepper

2.5 kg trout (a whole fish)
6 rashers streaky bacon
3 tablespoons lemon juice
extra 1/2 cup fresh parsley and dill
knob of butter

Preheat the oven to 200°C. To make the stuffing, fry the
leek and butter together in a frying pan over a low heat
until the leek softens. Add the bacon and cook until
browned. Stir in the breadcrumbs, parsley, dill, lemon
zest and juice. Remove from the heat and season with
salt and pepper.

   Place the trout on a flat surface and pack the stuffing
into the cavity. Stretch the bacon rashers over the cavity
to hold it together and wrap them around the trout. Oil
a baking dish and place the trout in it. Pour the lemon
juice over and scatter with the extra herbs and add the
knob of butter. Cover with aluminium foil and seal the
edges. Bake for 20–25 minutes until just cooked through.
To crisp the bacon, place the fish under a hot grill for 1–
2 minutes before serving. Alternatively, cook on a
barbecue, turning the parcel of fish over halfway through
the cooking process.

SERVES 4

Grated Potato Dauphinoise

1kg floury potatoes, peeled and washed
2 cloves garlic, peeled and grated
sea salt and freshly ground black pepper to taste
fresh flat-leaf parsley, chopped
4 tablespoons butter
1/2 cup grated parmesan cheese
2 cups cream

Grate the potatoes on a coarse grater. Toss the grated
potato with the grated garlic and season with salt and
pepper and parsley. Butter an ovenproof baking dish.
Lay one-third of the potato over the bottom of the dish
and then dot with one-third of the butter, and one-third
of the parmesan. Repeat this process twice more. Gently
pour the cream over and dot the top with butter. Bake in
an oven preheated to 180°C for about 40 minutes or
until the potato is golden.

SERVES 6

Butternut and Prosciutto Pie

DOUGH
$^1/_2$ teaspoon dried yeast
$^1/_4$ cup lukewarm water
pinch of sugar
2 cups plain flour
1 tablespoon olive oil
about $^1/_2$ cup lukewarm water
extra olive oil for oiling the bowl

FILLING
500g peeled butternut pumpkin, cooked
  and mashed
8 slices prosciutto
4 tablespoons toasted pine nuts
150g bocconcini, sliced
100g cow's feta, crumbled
2 cups fresh basil leaves

milk for glazing

Combine the yeast, water and pinch of sugar in a small bowl. Cover and leave in a warm place until frothy. Place the flour in a larger bowl and pour in the frothy yeast, the olive oil and enough of the second measure of lukewarm water into the flour to mix together to form a ball of dough. Transfer to a lightly floured surface and knead for 5–10 minutes until smooth. Place in a well-oiled bowl, cover with plastic food wrap and stand in a warm place until it doubles in size – about 1 hour.

When ready to proceed, preheat the oven to 225°C and grease a 30cm pizza pan. Knock down the dough and roll out half on a lightly floured surface into a circle large enough to fit the pizza pan. Spread the dough evenly with the mashed butternut, leaving a 1–2cm border around the edge. Lay the prosciutto, pine nuts, bocconcini, feta and basil on top. Brush the edge with a little water. Roll out the remaining dough to cover the top. Place carefully over the top and press the edges together to seal. Brush the top of the pie with a little milk and bake for 25 minutes until golden and crisp.

SERVES 8

Prosciutto-wrapped Salmon with Green Bean
and Tomato Salad

Prosciutto-wrapped Salmon

Carefully remove the fine 'pin' bones from the salmon, using tweezers.

6 x 200g salmon fillets, skinned and pin-boned
12 thin slices prosciutto
sea salt and freshly ground black pepper to taste
3 tablespoons avocado oil

Wrap the salmon fillets in the prosciutto (two slices per fillet) and season with salt and pepper. Place in a roasting pan and drizzle with avocado oil. Roast in an oven preheated to 220°C for about 10 minutes or until the prosciutto is golden. Serve with Green Bean and Tomato Salad (see below).

Green Bean and Tomato Salad

400g green beans (flat or round)
2 large tomatoes, skinned, quartered and
  deseeded
1 red onion, peeled and finely chopped
1 clove garlic, peeled and grated
3 tablespoons avocado oil
3 tablespoons lemon juice
2 tablespoons chopped fresh dill

Thinly slice flat beans, or top and tail round beans, then blanch, drain and dry and allow to cool. Toss together the beans, tomatoes and onion.

Combine the garlic, avocado oil, lemon juice and dill. Drizzle the dressing over the salad and toss together.

SERVES 6

Wood-roasted Salmon Cakes with Lime Mayonnaise

750g (about 7) floury potatoes, peeled and
    quartered
2 tablespoons sour cream
1 tablespoon butter
2 spring onions, finely chopped
200g wood-roasted or hot smoked salmon
1 teaspoon grated lemon rind
1 teaspoon lemon juice
1 tablespoon chopped fresh dill
1 egg
sea salt and freshly ground black pepper to taste
1$^1/_2$ cups fine fresh breadcrumbs
vegetable oil for frying
Lime Mayonnaise for serving (see below)

Cook the potatoes in salted boiling water until tender.
Drain and mash with the sour cream and butter. Stir in
the spring onions and set aside to cool. Remove the skin
from the salmon. Break the salmon into small pieces and
stir it into the mash along with the lemon rind, lemon
juice, dill, egg, salt and pepper. Take spoonfuls of the
mixture and shape into 18–20 salmon cakes. Roll in the
breadcrumbs. Heat the vegetable oil in a large frying pan,
and shallow-fry the cakes in batches over a medium heat.
Cook for 2–3 minutes each side or until golden brown.
Drain on kitchen paper and serve with Lime Mayonnaise.

SERVES 6

Lime Mayonnaise

4 egg yolks
1$^3/_4$ cups extra virgin olive oil
4–5 tablespoons lime juice
sea salt to taste

Place the egg yolks in a food processor or blender. With
the motor running, begin adding the olive oil drop by
drop, until the mixture thickens to form an emulsion.
Add a tablespoon of lime juice and continue to add the
olive oil in a slow, steady thin stream. Add extra lime
juice to taste and adjust the thickness. Season with salt.

MAKES 2 CUPS

Chicken, Avocado and Fennel Salad with Black Olive and Dried Tomato Dressing

A refreshing summer salad to have at the beach, on a picnic or just for a relaxing meal. Make the dressing first so it can be used as a marinade.

600g chicken breasts
olive oil
Black Olive and Dried Tomato Dressing (see below)
1 avocado, halved, stoned, peeled and sliced
1 fennel bulb, halved, cored and thinly sliced
3 cups salad greens of choice

Brush the chicken breasts with olive oil and barbecue or grill until tender and cooked. Allow to cool then slice into bite-sized pieces and place in a bowl. Pour half the Black Olive and Dried Tomato Dressing over the chicken and marinate for 1 hour. Layer the avocado, fennel and salad greens on a serving platter. Spoon the chicken over and gently toss together. Spoon the remaining dressing over and serve.

SERVES 6

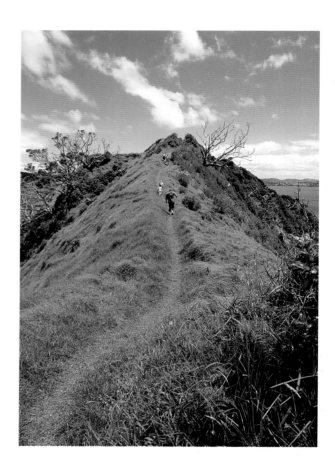

Black Olive and Dried Tomato Dressing

$^1/_4$ **cup kalamata olives, pitted and finely chopped**
$^1/_4$ **cup finely chopped sundried tomatoes**
$^1/_4$ **cup finely chopped chives**
1 tablespoon chopped fennel tips
$^1/_4$ **cup cider vinegar**
1 tablespoon olive oil
1 teaspoon grated lemon zest

Shake all the ingredients together in a jar.

MAKES ABOUT 1 CUP

Chicken, Avocado and Fennel Salad with Black Olive
and Dried Tomato Dressing

Oven-poached Cinnamon Quince

Oven-poached Cinnamon Quince

1¹/₂ litres water
¹/₄ cup lemon juice
1kg caster sugar
6 medium quinces
1 large cinnamon stick
runny cream or cream and mascarpone for serving

Place the water, lemon juice and sugar in a saucepan over a low heat and gently stir until the sugar dissolves. Peel, halve and core the quinces. Place them cut-side down in a single layer in a baking dish just large enough to hold them (you may need to use two dishes). Pour the syrup over the fruit and place the cinnamon stick in the dish. Seal the baking dish with aluminium foil and bake in an oven preheated to 180°C for 2 hours or until the quinces are tender and pink. Serve warm, drizzled with runny cream. Alternatively, mix a little pouring cream through some mascarpone until it's spreadable and serve on the side.

Variation

When the quinces are cooked, coarsely chop 1 cup of fresh walnuts or blanched almonds and combine with ¹/₂ cup of brown sugar. Remove the quinces from the syrup and arrange on a grill tray. Sprinkle the nut and sugar mixture evenly over the cut surfaces of the quinces. Place under a hot grill until the topping becomes bubbly and brown. Serve as described above.

SERVES 6

Rona Biscuits

These are named after a family friend who often leaves them on the doorstep for us. They are favourites with children – to make as well as to eat. Rolled thinner before cooking, they make crisp wafers to serve alongside ice cream.

125g butter, softened
100g (¹/₂ cup) sugar
150g (1¹/₄ cups) plain flour
¹/₂ teaspoon baking powder

Cream the butter and sugar in a bowl until pale and fluffy. Mix in the flour and baking powder. Roll into balls and place on a lightly buttered baking tray. Flatten with a fork. Bake in an oven preheated to 150°C for 12–15 minutes. Remove from the oven and transfer to a wire rack to cool.

Variations

Chocolate Rona Biscuits – add 1 tablespoon of cocoa with the flour.
Chocolate Chip Rona Biscuits – add 1 cup of chocolate chips with the flour.
Pistachio Rona Biscuits – add 1 cup coarsely chopped pistachio nuts with the flour.

MAKES 24

Rona Biscuits

Quince Jam

1kg quartered, peeled and cored quinces, cut
  into pieces or thinly sliced
about 7–8 cups water (enough to just cover
  the fruit)
1kg caster sugar
80ml lemon juice (about 2 juicy lemons)

Place the quince in a large heavy-bottomed saucepan
and just cover with the water. Put the lid on and bring
the fruit to boiling point. Adjust the heat and gently
simmer for 20 minutes or until the quince is tender.
Remove the saucepan from the heat and break up any
lumps with a potato masher. Add the sugar and lemon
juice and return the mixture to the heat, stirring
constantly until the sugar dissolves. Slowly return the jam
to a gentle simmer, uncovered. Regularly stir the jam to
prevent the mixture sticking. Skim off any scum that
forms on the surface. Begin testing the setting point (see
below) after simmering for 30 minutes. Ladle the jam
into clean, hot sterilised jars and seal. Store in a cool dry
place. Refrigerate after opening.

MAKES 5–6 CUPS

Jam Setting Test

*To test if jam has reached setting point, spoon a
little onto a chilled saucer and allow it to cool. The
jam is ready if a trail is left after you run your finger
through the jam and it wrinkles on the surface.*

Quick Tangy Marmalade

4 grapefruit
4 sweet oranges
4 litres water
3kg sugar

Wash the fruit, halve, and squeeze the juice. Reserve the
pips and tie them in a muslin bag. Place the grapefruit
and orange skins into a food processor and cut finely or
put them through a mincer. Place the juice, minced fruit,
bag of pips and water in a bowl and soak for 24 hours to
soften. Turn the mixture, including the bag of pips, into
a heavy-bottomed saucepan and simmer for 2 hours or
until the volume is reduced by half. Remove the bag of
pips and add the sugar. Stir over a low heat until the
sugar dissolves. Simmer rapidly for 20–30 minutes or until
the marmalade gels when tested. Remove from the heat,
skim and allow to cool slightly. Pour into clean, warm
sterilised jars and seal.

MAKES 10 CUPS

132

Peach and Nectarine Tart

$^1/_3$ cup caster sugar
$^1/_8$ cup water
4 white-fleshed peaches, quartered
4 nectarines, quartered
160g butter, softened
$^3/_4$ cup caster sugar
3 eggs
$^3/_4$ cup plain flour
1 cup ground almonds
whipped cream for serving

Place the caster sugar and water in a saucepan and stir together over a low heat until the sugar dissolves. Drop in the fruit and gently simmer until the fruit is soft but still holds its shape. Gently remove the fruit and set aside. Simmer the syrup for a further 5–10 minutes until it thickens slightly. Pour the syrup over the fruit and allow it to cool.

Preheat the oven to 180°C. Cream the butter and second measure of caster sugar together in a food processor until fluffy and pale. Add the eggs one at a time until well combined. Add the flour and ground almonds and pulse until blended. Spoon the mixture into a 23–25cm tart flan, and spread it evenly. Bake for 25–30 minutes or until golden and just firm. Allow to stand for 10 minutes, then remove from the tart tin to a serving plate. While the base is still warm, arrange the fruit over the base and spoon over a little syrup. Serve the tart with whipped cream with a little more syrup swirled through the cream.

SERVES 8

Caramel and Chocolate Slice

Pack this as an indulgent sweet treat in the picnic or for an outdoor excursion.

BASE
1 cup self-raising flour, sifted
1 cup ground almonds
1 cup brown sugar
160g butter, melted

TOPPING
380g can store-bought caramelised condensed milk
125g good-quality dark chocolate
30g butter

Preheat the oven to 180°C. Combine the flour, ground almonds and sugar in a bowl. Pour in the butter and stir to combine. Press the mixture into a 20cm x 30cm buttered lamington pan. Bake for 10–15 minutes until golden. While the base is still warm, pour in the caramelised condensed milk and spread it evenly over the base. Allow to cool. Combine the chocolate and butter and stir together over a low heat until melted and combined. Pour the chocolate topping over the caramel and spread evenly. Allow to cool, then refrigerate until set. Cut into squares or bars.

MAKES ABOUT 40 BARS

Peach and Nectarine Tart

glossary

Al dente – an Italian phrase meaning 'to the tooth' used to describe pasta that when cooked offers a slight resistance when bitten into.

Allspice – a pea-size berry off the pimento tree which is dried to a dark brown and can be purchased whole or ground.

Avocado Oil – an oil extracted by cold pressing the flesh of the avocado. Great for basting meat, fish and chicken while cooking, or for use in salad dressings or dipping bread.

Bain-Marie – a French term for a water bath. This method of cooking involves placing a container (pan, bowl, soufflé dish) of food in a large shallow pan of warm water, which surrounds the food with gentle heat.

Birds Eye Chilli – a small red or orange chilli originating from East Africa.

Bocconcini – small fresh balls of Italian mozzarella, usually made from cow's milk and sold in water or brine.

Borlotti Beans – also known as saligna beans, they come from Italy. They are tan in colour and cook to a creamy consistency in casseroles, dips and salads.

Broad Bean Kernels – also known as fava beans. When you blanch the seed and peel back the skin you expose the inside or inner kernel.

Broccolini – a variety of broccoli sold in small bunches.

Bundt Tin – originally the trademark name of a tube pan with fluted sides, it is now the general name of any cake tin of that style. Because of the fluted sides it needs to be greased well.

Celeriac – a knobbly brown bulb of a root vegetable which, when peeled, has a creamy flesh and tastes like a cross between celery and parsley.

Chorizo – a highly seasoned, coarsely ground pork sausage flavoured with garlic, chilli and various other spices.

To Cream – to beat a combination of ingredients, often butter and sugar, until the mixture is soft, smooth and creamy.

Dijon Mustard – originated in Dijon, France, a pale greyish yellow mustard known for its clean sharp flavour. Made from brown mustard seeds, white wine and unfermented grape juice.

Extra Virgin Olive Oil – a cold pressed olive oil resulting from the first pressing of the olives, therefore having a low level of acidity. It is considered the finest, fruitiest and most intense in flavour.

Gem Irons – usually made from cast iron, gem irons come in trays of 12–24 small oblong-shaped pockets like muffin pans.

Kalamata Olives – a variety of olive, purple-black in colour with the classic bitter olive flavour. They are often split to allow the wine-vinegar marinade in which they are soaked to penetrate the flesh.

Mascarpone – a cheese hailing from Italy's Lombardy region. It is a buttery-rich double cream to triple cream cheese made from cow's milk. Its ivory colour is soft and delicate and ranges in texture from light clotted cream to that of butter at room temperature.

Mozzarella – originally an Italian cheese made from buffalo's milk, this soft white curd cheese has a mild delicate flavour and is usually shaped into small or larger balls. Delicious eaten raw but also known for its wonderful melting qualities.

Orzo – rice-shaped pasta.

Pancetta – Italian bacon, cured with salt and spiced – but not smoked. It comes in a sausage-shaped roll and is available from specialty food stores and some supermarkets.

Parmesan – a hard dry cheese made from skimmed or partially skimmed cow's milk. It has a rich sharp flavour with a golden rind and straw coloured interior.

Pecorino Cheese – a hard dry cheese originally made in Italy from sheep's milk. It comes in large cylinders with a hard yellow crust and yellow white interior. Usually sold in wedges in the supermarket.

Pin-bone – to remove the very fine bones from a fish fillet, such as salmon, using tweezers.

Portobello Mushrooms – a cultivated flat mushroom cap with brown flesh.

Prosciutto – Italian ham, it is seasoned, salt cured and air dried. The meat is then pressed which produces a firm dense texture.

Quince – a fragrant, yellow skinned, old fashioned fruit which tastes like a cross between an apple and a pear. The hard yellow flesh is dry and astringent. When cooked it transforms into a ruby coloured tender delight.

Ricotta – an Italian fresh unripened cheese made from the whey of cow's milk or sometimes sheep's milk. It should be smooth and milky tasting.

Rocket – a bitterish aromatic peppery green leaf for use in salads and pesto. Also called Arugula.

Savoy Cabbage – a mellow flavoured cabbage with a loose head of crinkled leaves.

Sea Salt – a natural salt which occurs as the result of the evaporation of sea water. It comes in fine or coarse crystals.

Shanghai Cabbage – a variety of bok choy with a white stalk and tender green leaves – it resembles a bunch of wide-stalked celery with long full leaves.

Shiitake Mushrooms – originally a Japanese mushroom with a dark brown cap and tan striations. Its meaty flesh has a full-bodied bosky flavour.

Smoked Paprika – fresh capsicum is oak smoked which also dries it. It is ground and used to flavour stews, sauces and marinades.

NZ/AUSTRALIA	US	GREAT BRITAIN
Beetroot	beet	beetroot
Capsicum	bell pepper	pepper
Caster sugar	superfine sugar	caster sugar
Cornflour	cornstarch	cornflour
Cream (NZ)	whipping cream	whipping cream
Eggplant	eggplant	aubergine
Ginger Nuts	Ginger Snaps	Ginger Nuts
Golden syrup	corn syrup	golden syrup
Grill	broil	grill
Icing sugar	confectioner's sugar	icing sugar
Minced beef	ground beef	minced beef
Plain flour	all-purpose flour	plain flour
Prawn	shrimp	prawn
Rock melon	cantaloupe	cantaloupe or musk melon
Self-raising flour	self-rising flour	self-raising flour
Sultanas	seedless white raisins	sultanas
Tasty cheese	cheddar or jack cheese	cheddar cheese
Tomato paste	tomato paste	tomato purée
Zucchini	zucchini	courgette

weights & measures

Abbreviations

g	gram
kg	kilogram
mm	millimetre
cm	centimetre
ml	millilitre
°C	degrees Celsius

Weight conversions

NZ METRIC	IMPERIAL/US
25g	1 oz
50g	2 oz
75g	3 oz
100g	$3^{1}/_{2}$ oz
125g	$4^{1}/_{2}$ oz
150g	5 oz
175g	6 oz
200g	7 oz
225g	8 oz
250g	9 oz
275g	$9^{1}/_{2}$ oz
300g	$10^{1}/_{2}$ oz
325g	$11^{1}/_{2}$ oz
350g	$12^{1}/_{2}$ oz
375g	13 oz
400g	14 oz
450g	16 oz (1 lb)
500g	$17^{1}/_{2}$ oz
750g	$26^{1}/_{2}$ oz
1 kg	35 oz ($2^{1}/_{4}$ lb)

Length conversions

METRIC	IMPERIAL/US
0.5cm (5mm)	$^{1}/_{4}$ inch
1cm	$^{1}/_{2}$ inch
2.5cm	1 inch
5cm	2 inches
10cm	4 inches
20cm	8 inches
30cm	12 inches (1 foot)

Liquid conversions

NZ METRIC	IMPERIAL	US
5ml (1 teaspoon)	$^{1}/_{4}$ fl oz	1 teaspoon
15ml (1 tablespoon)	$^{1}/_{2}$ fl oz	1 tablespoon
30ml ($^{1}/_{8}$ cup)	1 fl oz	$^{1}/_{8}$ cup
60ml ($^{1}/_{4}$ cup)	2 fl oz	$^{1}/_{4}$ cup
125ml ($^{1}/_{2}$ cup)	4 fl oz	$^{1}/_{2}$ cup
150ml	5 fl oz ($^{1}/_{4}$ pint)	$^{2}/_{3}$ cup
175ml	6 fl oz	$^{3}/_{4}$ cup
250ml (1 cup)	8 fl oz	1 cup ($^{1}/_{2}$ pint)
300ml	10 fl oz ($^{1}/_{2}$ pint)	$1^{1}/_{4}$ cups
375ml	12 fl oz	$1^{1}/_{2}$ cups
500ml (2 cups)	16 fl oz	2 cups (1 pint)
600ml	20 fl oz (1 pint)	$2^{1}/_{2}$ cups

NB The Australian metric tablespoon measures 20ml

Temperature conversions

CELSIUS	FAHRENHEIT	GAS
100°C	225°F	$^1/_4$
125°C	250°F	$^1/_2$
150°C	300°F	2
160°C	325°F	3
170°C	325°F	3
180°C	350°F	4
190°C	375°F	5
200°C	400°F	6
210°C	425°F	7
220°C	425°F	7
230°C	450°F	8
250°C	500°F	9

Cake tin sizes

METRIC	IMPERIAL/US
15cm	6 inches
18cm	7 inches
20cm	8 inches
23cm	9 inches
25cm	10 inches
28cm	11 inches

index

acknowledgements

As always with a project like this there are many individuals who deserve special thanks.

To Renée Lang and the entire team at New Holland – thank you so much for the wonderful support. I congratulate Barbara Nielsen and Alison Dench for their superb editing skills; Christine Hansen, who has again excelled herself with her stunning book design; and my co-author Ian Batchelor, who brings my food to life with his mouth-watering images.

Penny Oliver

I received so much enthusiastic help that I hardly know where to start. Thanks to Steve and Penny Bicknell of the Maruia River Lodge, Shenandoah, Murchison for sharing the tranquil beauty of their lodge and its magical surrounds; Mike Buchanan, the expert fishing guide from Coch-y-Bondhu Lodge, Murchison; and the friends and family who put up with me and the camera and who deserve more than thanks – but they are not going to get it.

Thanks also to those people who helped enormously without even knowing. You may find that it's you tramping off into the distance, pictured with a fishing rod, or guiding a pony over a fence.

Lastly my co-author, Penny Oliver, is always fun to work with and prepares food beautifully. I photograph it...and then sample it. If the photographs convey to you even a fraction of how delicious the food is then you'll understand how much I enjoy my work.

Ian Batchelor

suppliers

Country Road Homewares, Newmarket, Auckland
Albertine – bowls and plates, Ponsonby Road, Auckland
Red Current – plates and crockery, Ponsonby Road, Auckland
Superb Herb Company Ltd